IMMERSION
Bible Studies

REVELATION

Praise for IMMERSION

"IMMERSION BIBLE STUDIES is a powerful tool in helping readers to hear God speak through Scripture and to experience a deeper faith as a result."
Adam Hamilton, author of *24 Hours That Changed the World*

"This unique Bible study makes Scripture come alive for students. Through the study, students are invited to move beyond the head into the heart of faith."
Bishop Joseph W. Walker, author of *Love and Intimacy*

"This beautiful series helps readers become fluent in the words and thoughts of God, for purposes of illumination, strength building, and developing a closer walk with the One who loves us so."
Laurie Beth Jones, author of *Jesus, CEO* and *The Path*

"I highly commend to you IMMERSION BIBLE STUDIES, which tells us what the Bible teaches and how to apply it personally."
John Ed Mathison, author of *Treasures of the Transformed Life*

"The IMMERSION BIBLE STUDIES series is no less than a game changer. It ignites the purpose and power of Scripture by showing us how to do more than just know God or love God; it gives us the tools to love like God as well."
Shane Stanford, author of *You Can't Do Everything . . . So Do Something*

IMMERSION
Bible Studies

REVELATION

Henry G. Brinton and John Yueh-Han Yieh

Abingdon Press

Nashville

REVELATION
IMMERSION BIBLE STUDIES
by Henry G. Brinton and John Yueh-Han Yieh

Copyright © 2011 by Abingdon Press

Library of Congress Cataloging-in-Publication Data

Brinton, Henry G., 1960-
    Revelation / Henry G. Brinton and John Yueh-Han Yieh.
        p.   cm.—(Immersion Bible studies)
    978-1-4267-0992-0 (alk. paper)
    1. Bible. N.T. Revelation—Textbooks.   I. Yieh, John Yueh-Han.   II. Title.
    BS2825.55.B75 2011
    228'.077—dc23

                                                                    2011019626

Editor: Stan Purdum
Leader Guide Writer: John P. "Jack" Gilbert

11 12 13 14 15 16 17 18 19 20—10 9 8 7 6 5 4 3 2 1

Manufactured in the United States of America

Contents

IMMERSION BIBLE STUDIES 7

1. God Cares! 9

2. Wonder, Love, and Praise 19

3. Victory Belongs to God 29

4. The Endurance of the Saints 39

5. God's Judgments Are Just 49

6. Loose and Extravagant Ways 59

7. God Is in Control 69

8. All Things New 79

Leader Guide 89

REVIEW TEAM

Diane Blum
Pastor
East End United Methodist Church
Nashville, Tennessee

Susan Cox
Pastor
McMurry United Methodist Church
Claycomo, Missouri

Margaret Ann Crain
Professor of Christian Education
Garrett-Evangelical Theological Seminary
Evanston, Illinois

Nan Duerling
Curriculum Writer and Editor
Cambridge, Maryland

Paul Escamilla
Pastor and Writer
St. John's United Methodist Church
Austin, Texas

James Hawkins
Pastor and Writer
Smyrna, Delaware

Andrew Johnson
Professor of New Testament
Nazarene Theological Seminary
Kansas City, Missouri

Snehlata Patel
Pastor
Woodrow United Methodist Church
Staten Island, New York

Emerson B. Powery
Professor of New Testament
Messiah College
Grantham, Pennsylvania

Clayton Smith
Pastoral Staff
Church of the Resurrection
Leawood, Kansas

Harold Washington
Professor of Hebrew Bible
Saint Paul School of Theology
Kansas City, Missouri

Carol Wehrheim
Curriculum Writer and Editor
Princeton, New Jersey

IMMERSION BIBLE STUDIES

A fresh new look at the Bible, from beginning to end,
and what it means in your life.

Welcome to IMMERSION!

We've asked some of the leading Bible scholars, teachers, and pastors to help us with a new kind of Bible study. IMMERSION remains true to Scripture but always asks, "Where are you in your life? What do you struggle with? What makes you rejoice?" Then it helps you read the Scriptures to discover their deep, abiding truths. IMMERSION is about God and God's Word, and it is also about you—not just your thoughts, but your feelings and your faith.

In each study you will prayerfully read the Scripture and reflect on it. Then you will engage it in three ways:

Claim Your Story

Through stories and questions, think about your life, with its struggles and joys.

Enter the Bible Story

Explore Scripture and consider what God is saying to you.

Live the Story

Reflect on what you have discovered, and put it into practice in your life.

IMMERSION makes use of an exciting new translation of Scripture, the Common English Bible (CEB). The CEB and IMMERSION BIBLE STUDIES will offer adults:

- the emotional expectation to find the love of God
- the rational expectation to find the knowledge of God
- reliable, genuine, and credible power to transform lives
- clarity of language

Whether you are using the Common English Bible or another translation, IMMERSION BIBLE STUDIES will offer a refreshing plunge into God's Word, your life, and your life with God.

1

God Cares!

Revelation 1–3

Claim Your Story

Where were you on September 11, 2001? Most of us can remember exactly what we were doing when we first learned of the brutal terrorist attacks on the World Trade Center, Pentagon, and Flight 93 over Pennsylvania. The shock and sadness of that day will stay with us for many years, and it certainly set the tone for the first decade of the twenty-first century.

The several years following that horrible day brought a series of natural disasters and human calamities. The tsunami in the Indian Ocean and earthquake in Haiti devoured tens of thousands of lives. The crisis in the housing market and crash of the banking system exposed human greed and corporate deception and caused many people to lose jobs, savings, houses, and self-esteem. The earthquake, tsunami, and nuclear disaster in Japan did tremendous damage to thousands of human beings and the environment.

Most troubling about these calamities is the suffering of innocent people, including passengers who lost their lives on Flight 93 and homeowners who lost their houses even though they worked hard and played by the rules. We wonder why they suffer, while the wicked who caused the troubles continue to prosper. The scales of justice seem to be out of balance.

Perhaps you sense that a destructive force is impacting your life, community, and environment; but you cannot seem to control or defeat it. You want to know where God is. Is God in charge? Doesn't God care?

Enter the Bible Story

To many people wrestling with these heart-wrenching questions of "theodicy" (justice of God), the Book of Revelation provides a series of visions from Jesus Christ to reassure believers of God's power and care. These visions came to a servant of Christ named John, the author of Revelation (1:1). John was a pastor, with concern for "the seven churches that are in Asia" (1:4), and also a prophetic spokesperson for God. Probably not the same John who wrote the Gospel of John, he was most likely a leader of the church who was exiled to the island of Patmos for refusing to address the Roman emperor Domitian (served as emperor from A.D. 81–96) as "Lord and God" (1:9).

Yes, promises John in a time of hardship, God is firmly in charge; and God cares deeply for us. We will be filled with hope and given power to endure any afflictions if we can hear and see what God is doing. At the beginning of the book, John is keen to show the readers how eagerly God wants to reveal God's plans for the world.

Like us, John and the seven churches in Asia Minor were struggling with senseless suffering in the world that raised serious doubts about God's justice and mercy. The last decade of the first century was a tough time, an age of angst, for everybody in the Roman Empire. Brutal civil wars had wrecked the peace and order of the Empire and damaged its food production and commercial trade. People were desperate to survive political oppression and economic exploitation, as well as natural disasters, social injustice, and human atrocities. Then, as today, earthquakes, famines, plagues, robberies, and violence afflicted entire nations.

The Imperial Cult

Christians in the province of Asia Minor suffered even more miseries than other citizens because of their robust belief in Jesus Christ as Lord and their critical attitude toward the politics and religious practices of the larger society. In order to consolidate the Roman emperor's absolute authority and ensure strong social cohesion, an imperial cult (worship of the emperor as the patron god of the Roman Empire) had been established. Participating in the imperial cult became a test of political allegiance rather than a matter of personal religious freedom. Those who refused to participate were suspected of treason and subjected to severe punishment, especially under the emperors Nero and Domitian.

In that social-political climate, John and his fellow Christians collided head-on with local authorities. They honored Jesus Christ as the only divine Lord and refused to partake in the imperial cult's celebrations. As a result, John and his churches were put under disparaging social pressure from provincial agents of the imperial cult and were vulnerable to the charge of disloyalty. Even though there was no widespread official persecution of Christians for their religious faith (as took place under Emperor Decius), they suffered economic as well as social consequences.

Although we do not face an imperial cult in twenty-first-century America, we certainly feel pressure to conform to the standards being set by Washington, Madison Avenue, and Hollywood—all of which have an impact on our politics, our buying habits, and our sexual behavior.

Caesar or Christ?

Confronted by the choice of Emperor Caesar or Lord Jesus Christ, some leaders in John's churches chose to defy the idolatrous imperial cult and worship only one God and one Lord—even if it meant colliding with local authorities. For them, worshiping Caesar was a violation of the most foundational confession of faith in God and the Lord Jesus Christ. The imperial cult included not only political beliefs and religious rituals but also ethical values and moral practices, many of which were not in harmony with the principles of the Christian faith.

For many Christians, there was no room for compromise; and they were willing to pay a high price for keeping their faith intact. Antipas of Pergamum was martyred (Revelation 2:13), and John was banished to the isle of Patmos as a prisoner (1:9). Other church leaders, recognizing their

minority status in a hostile world, tried to get along with the Roman powers. They tolerated the eating of food that had been offered to idols and
sexual immorality, as well as other activities related to the practices of the
imperial cult and the popular ways of the dominant culture.

John disapproved of the views of these leaders and worried about corruption in the community of faith, so he labeled them "Balaam" (Revelation 2:14) and "Jezebel" (2:20). These were two infamous figures in the
Old Testament who harmed God's people and were punished for their sins.
To respond to social harassment, John's churches had to decide how to
act as Christians in an anti-Christian culture. They faced questions that
are still with us today: Is it wise to endure avoidable hardship for the sake
of faithfulness? Is it possible to make Christian faith acceptable to the
world? Which is preferable, fidelity to a core value or adaptation to
a changing reality?

A Vision of God's Plan

John made his choice and endured the consequences on Patmos.
Although well aware that Christians were experiencing hardship at the
hands of Caesar's agents, he was convinced that God saw their suffering
and cared deeply about their oppression. Knowing that God had heard
the cry of the Israelites and brought them out of Egypt, John believed that
a merciful God would neither permit God's people to be tempted and
tested endlessly nor allow evil to afflict the innocent forever. Then and
now, God has a plan and a message for faithful believers, as well as a warning for those who are drifting away. One day soon, all that is evil and
imperfect will be destroyed; and there will be peace and joy in a new
heaven and new earth.

To show John the plan and the message, God granted him a rare
glimpse of the divine court in heaven and a series of visions for the future
before ordering him to write down what he had seen and heard for the
churches. Like Enoch and Daniel, John was given a heavenly vision; and
like them, he was frightened, excited, and inspired by what he witnessed.
This extraordinary experience in the Spirit bolstered his confidence and
re-energized him.

Old Testament Roots of Revelation Imagery

Balaam, a greedy false prophet	Numbers 22:4b-6 "Balak, Zippor's son, was king of Moab at that time. He sent messengers to Balaam...to summon him: 'A people has come out of Egypt, and they have now covered the land. They have settled next to me. Now please come and curse this people for me because they are stronger than I am.'"	Revelation 2:14 "But I have a few things against you, because you have some there who follow Balaam's teaching. Balaam had taught Balak to trip up the Israelites so that they would eat food sacrificed to idols and commit sexual immorality."
Jezebel, a wicked, idolatrous queen	1 Kings 21:25-26 "Truly there has never been anyone like Ahab who sold out by doing evil in the LORD's eyes—evil that his wife Jezebel led him to do. Ahab's actions were deplorable. He followed after the worthless idols exactly like the Amorites had done—the very ones the LORD had removed before the Israelites."	Revelation 2:20 "But I have this against you: you put up with that woman, Jezebel, who calls herself a prophet. You allow her to teach and to mislead my servants into committing sexual immorality and eating food sacrificed to idols."
Son of Man, or "Human One"	Daniel 7:13-14 "As I continued to watch this night vision of mine, I suddenly saw / one like a human being / coming with the heavenly clouds. / He came to the ancient one / and was presented before him. / Rule, glory and kingship / were given to him; / all peoples, nations, and languages / will serve him. / His rule is an everlasting one— / it will never pass away!— / his kingship is indestructible."	Revelation 1:13-14 "In the middle of the lampstands I saw someone who looked like the Human One. He wore a robe that stretched down to his feet, and he had a golden sash around his chest. His head and hair were white as white wool—like snow—and his eyes were like a fiery flame."

John believed Jesus Christ to be the Lamb of God who redeemed the world and also the Son of Man who mediated God's eschatological (end of time) plan. Because of this, John called his letter "A revelation of Jesus Christ, which God gave him to show his servants what must soon take place" (Revelation 1:1). To call his letter "revelation" (apocalypse) is to say it is a disclosure of divine truths previously hidden or unknown. To say the revelation is "of Jesus" is to suggest that its contents concern Jesus' role in God's plan and that it was issued by Jesus. God's messages revealed by Jesus are always credible and worthy of prayerful attention.

Who Is Jesus Christ?

Since the revelation is "of Jesus Christ," John gives a long introduction to him in his greeting to the seven churches. Jesus Christ is "the faithful witness, the firstborn from among the dead, and the ruler of the kings of the earth" (Revelation 1:5). This refers to Jesus' death, resurrection, and exaltation—the three most important aspects of his mission of redemption for humankind and his revelation of God's love. It also reminds the readers of how Jesus' witness by martyrdom has earned him the honor of being the pioneer of resurrection and has given him authority over all kings of the world. The relevance to us and to the first readers of Revelation is clear: Be faithful to the crucified, risen, and reigning Lord. Even if you have to endure hardships for Jesus in a hostile culture, you will be highly rewarded by God, just as Christ has been. And do not be intimidated by agents of the worldly empire because Jesus Christ your Lord is ruling over all the kings of the world.

John also praises Jesus Christ as the one who has loved us; freed us from our sins; and made us "a kingdom, priests to his God and Father" (Revelation 1:6). Our sins have been forgiven by the loving Christ with his sacrificial blood; so we are cleansed and made ready to serve God as "a kingdom of priests," just as the Hebrew slaves were released from the bondage of Pharaoh to worship the only true God (Exodus 19:6). By reminding the readers of their sanctified status as the "kingdom" and "priests" of God, John may have intended to encourage them to live a holy life in honor of God, against the Roman Empire and its imperial priests. No one, not even Caesar, can defy God's lordship or enslave God's priests with intimidation or temptation.

High Priest and Divine Warrior

To show his deep concern for the seven churches, Jesus personally delivered his messages (Revelation 1:9–3:22). Christ's majestic appearance was so awesome that John was frightened half to death. He says that Jesus looked like "the Son of Man" (NRSV) or "the Human One" (CEB) (1:13), a term that in the Book of Daniel describes the divine being in the form of a human being who was to come to judge the world on the day of the Lord (Daniel 7:13-14). Jesus was dressed in a long robe with a golden sash, the attire of the high priest. He had white hair, fiery eyes, brass feet, and a sharp sword in his mouth—the figure of a divine warrior. "His appearance was like the sun shining with all its power" (1:13-16).

Christian artists such as Albrecht Dürer and William Blake have tried to depict this terrifying vision in paintings, and it is clear that this image of Jesus is starkly different from the gentle Jesus of Nazareth. It reveals Jesus' role as the powerful Lord who is coming to judge the world, starting with his churches. But this vision of Jesus as High Priest and Divine Warrior is also meant to reassure John's churches. The Roman Empire may terrorize people with swords, but Jesus Christ has overcome death and holds "the keys of Death and the Grave" (Revelation 1:18); so Christians need not be scared at all. The vision of Jesus standing in the middle of the seven lampstands means that he is present with the seven churches, watching over them—just as he is with us.

What Are Christ's Messages?

The revelation of Jesus Christ is "prophecy" (a message from God), and those who listen and keep it will receive divine favor (Revelation 1:3). According to individual conditions, Jesus issues specific messages to each of the seven churches.

About the Scripture

The Messages to the Seven Churches

Location	Praise	Censure	Challenge	Command
Ephesus	Endure, resist evildoers, test false apostles, and suffer for Jesus	Lose original love	Nicolaitans	Change hearts and lives, do what they did at first
Smyrna	Hardship, poverty		"Satan's throne," slander by Jews, prison, martyrdom	Be not afraid, be faithful
Pergamum	Faithful	Follow Balaam's teaching (idol food, sexual immorality)	Antipas martyred, Balaam, Nicolaitans	Change hearts and lives
Thyatira	Love, faithfulness, service, endurance	Accept Jezebel (sexual immorality, idol food)	Jezebel, her followers will be punished	Change hearts and lives, hold on to what they have
Sardis	A few are not stained	Dead		Wake up, remember, hold on, and change hearts and lives
Philadelphia	Keep the word, do not deny Jesus		Satan's synagogue	Hold on
Laodicea		Lukewarm, miserable, poor, blind, naked		Be earnest, change hearts and lives, open the door

All seven churches were facing social harassment, the martyrdom of Antipas in Pergamum being the most serious case. Some were also slandered by the Jewish synagogues. Most of the churches were endangered by internal crises, their lives tainted by pagan culture and their practice misled by false teachers. So, while praising their faithful endurance, Jesus also urged them to repent and to restore their original love for God and him.

Their problems—political oppression, religious discrimination, false leadership, and corrupted lifestyle—continue to test our churches today. Jesus calls us to do battle with these problems, urging us to hold firm, endure patiently, and emerge victorious (Revelation 2:7b, 11b, 17b, 26; 3:5, 12, 21). Their responses to these problems—apostasy, adaptation, endurance, and martyrdom—can also serve as important teaching tools for us today. At the end of each letter, Jesus repeats an appeal that echoes to the present day: "If you can hear, listen to what the Spirit is saying to the churches" (2:7a, 11a, 17a, 29; 3:6, 13, 22).

How Can We Understand and Share These Messages?

John was able to receive the messages to the churches because he was a faithful servant of Christ, testifying to Jesus without fear. He was willing to share with the churches in the "hardship, kingdom, and endurance" (Revelation 1:9). While suffering banishment on Patmos, he kept hope alive by maintaining the spiritual disciplines of prayer and worship; so he was ready to see Jesus when he appeared with divine messages on the Lord's day. John's virtues of faith, love, and hope made it possible for him to hear and share the messages of Jesus.

The same is true for us. Our willingness to suffer along with fellow Christians will give us credibility in the community of faith and enable us to share the message of a caring God. The disciplines of prayer and worship give us access to what Jesus is saying to us today. And when we speak out of faith, hope, and love, people will hear the words of correction and encouragement that Jesus wants us to share.

Live the Story

God knows the hardships we are experiencing as residents of a world controlled by ideologies, customs, and politics inimical to God. When confronted by evils such as the September 11 terrorist attacks, we are bound to feel fear, anxiety, frustration, and disillusionment. But God will not leave us suffering as helpless orphans or allow wicked people and evil systems to oppress and exploit us forever. God has planned a bright future for us and for the world, and this plan is already in motion. God is in charge, and God cares deeply for us.

How do you see yourself maintaining the spiritual disciplines of prayer and worship, which Revelation 1–3 recommends for the living of a faithful, loving, and hopeful life in the middle of hardship? The promise of these chapters is that you can remain connected to the Lord Jesus Christ, in communion with all the saints, both past and present. You can encourage your fellow Christians as you listen to what the Spirit is saying to the church and share insights into how to practice virtue and avoid vice. With the support and accountability of the Christian community, you can live a victorious life, confident that a powerful and caring God is always working to save you.

Wonder, Love, and Praise

Revelation 4–5

Claim Your Story

We live in a "culture of disbelief," according to Stephen Carter, a professor of law at Yale University, one that prefers religion never to be heard and rarely seen. And yet our culture has its gods. Scientists adore knowledge, politicians revere power, and CEOs worship money. We see the rotten fruits of such idol worship when ethics are ignored in research experiments, reputations are destroyed in political campaigns, and honesty is sacrificed on the altar of profit.

When these idols take center stage, the living God is pushed to the edges of our lives. God becomes a mere comforter, a false god who endorses our desires rather than the Creator and Redeemer who has an absolute claim on us. Sadly, when the one true God is replaced or marginalized, the innocent are injured and the poor are forgotten. Social justice is ignored, and the environment is abused.

Religion finds its proper place in the traditions of group worship. At its best, this is a public activity in which God is encountered and people are filled with wonder, love, and praise. So what happens when you catch a glimpse of the glory of almighty God? How is your life transformed by the experience of joining the angels in praise and worship of the Creator?

Enter the Bible Story

Immediately after Jesus appears to John and reveals his messages to the seven churches (Revelation 1–3), John is summoned to "come up" to heaven to see "what must take place after this" (4:1). To make a divine revelation clear, God has come in the form of Jesus and spoken in a language we can understand, as spelled out in the seven letters. But now, in order for us to appreciate the divine plan for the future, we need to be lifted up to the presence of God so that we can see things from a heavenly perspective.

John is lifted up to heaven in the Spirit. The Common English Bible translates *en pneumati* as "in a Spirit-inspired trance" (Revelation 4:2). This does not necessarily mean that John went through a shamanistic experience that involved loss of consciousness or some sort of hallucination that we might describe in medical terms. In his mysterious trip to heaven, he seems self-aware, able to converse with angels, and able to remember the details of what he sees, like Ezekiel the prophet (Ezekiel 1–3). Most important is his claim that this extraordinary experience is inspired by the Spirit of God.

God works in mysterious ways and communicates to different people in different ways—by laws, prophecies, or visions seen by prophets and apostles in the Bible. What is certain is that God is willing to open the door to heaven for us so that we may come into God's presence. Guided by the power of the Holy Spirit, we can gain an understanding of God's plan.

The experience of John teaches us that worship has a role to play in God's communication with us, leading us to wonder why God allowed John to witness the solemn worship in the heavenly court (Revelation 4–5) before showing him the visions of future events (Revelation 6–22). And how is worship related to the hardship of the church and the destiny of the world? To answer these questions, we need to consider what John sees and hears in that heavenly worship.

Court

John sees the colorful and majestic court in heaven and is mesmerized. Almighty God, looking like jasper and carnelian, is seated on a throne at the center of the court, enclosed by an emeraldlike rainbow. The throne is encircled by four living creatures with many watchful eyes, which are in turn surrounded by twenty-four white-clothed elders and their thrones. The throne of God is at the center of two concentric circles of worshipers. In the inner circle are four magnificent creatures with eyes and wings whose resemblance to lion, ox, human being, and eagle represent the most powerful creatures in four spheres of the world (Revelation 4:7). In the outer circle are the twenty-four elders representing the twelve tribes of Israel and the twelve disciples of Jesus—people from the Old Testament and the New Testament worshiping God together.

With its central location in the court, the throne is a natural focal point. As a symbol of kingship and power, it proclaims the message that God reigns over the universe. The throne's majesty is visual (lightning) as well as aural (voices and thunder), similar to what Moses and Elijah saw and heard with trembling fear in the presence of God (Exodus 20:18-21; 1 Kings 19:11-18). In front of the throne, seven flaming torches, symbolizing the seven spirits of God, stand ready to serve. Finally, a crystal-like glass sea separates the throne from John. As in Ezekiel's vision of God (Ezekiel 1), the almighty God in Revelation 4:2-7 is both majestic and holy.

Worship

The members of the heavenly court throw their entire bodies into worship. The winged living creatures unceasingly sing "holy, holy, holy" to praise "the Lord God Almighty, who was and is and is coming" (Revelation 4:8), as was once witnessed by the prophet Isaiah (Isaiah 6). In sync with them, the twenty-four elders fall down before the throne, worship the eternal God, and throw down their crowns to pay homage to God, saying in unison that God is worthy "to receive glory and honor and power" because God created all things (4:10-11). This vision of heavenly worship teaches us that the focus of worship should never be anything but our almighty and holy God. Proper liturgy should lead people to honor God with songs of praise and to confess that God is nothing less than the one who creates and renews all things.

Across the Testaments

Visions of Heaven in the Old and New Testaments

Court	Ezekiel 1:4-5 "As I watched, suddenly a driving storm came out of the north, a great cloud flashing fire, with brightness all around. At its center, in the middle of the fire, there was something like gleaming amber. And inside that were forms of four living creatures."	Revelation 4:5-6 "From the throne came lightning, voices, and thunder.... In the center, by the throne, were four living creatures encircling the throne."
Worship	Isaiah 6:2-3 "Winged creatures were stationed around [God]. Each had six wings: with two they veiled their faces, with two their feet, and with two they flew about. They shouted to each other, saying: / 'Holy, holy, holy is the LORD of heavenly forces! / All the earth is filled with God's glory!'"	Revelation 4:8 "Each of the four living creatures had six wings, and each was covered all around and on the inside with eyes. They never rest day or night, but keep on saying, / 'Holy, holy, holy / is the Lord God Almighty, / who was and is and is coming.'"
God	Exodus 3:14 "God said to Moses, 'I Am Who I Am. So say to the Israelites, "I Am has sent me to you."'"	Revelation 4:10 "The twenty-four elders fall before the one seated on the throne. They worship the one who lives forever and ever."
Christ	Genesis 49:9 "Judah is a lion's cub; from the prey, my son, you rise up." Isaiah 11:1 A shoot will grow up from the stump of Jesse; / a branch will sprout from his roots."	Revelation 5:5 "Then one of the elders said to me, 'Don't weep. Look! The Lion of the tribe of Judah, the Root of David, has emerged victorious so that he can open the scroll and its seven seals.'"

God

What does this vision reveal to us about God? You might be surprised to discover, despite a detailed description of the magnificent heavenly court, that God's appearance is never revealed, in accordance with the second commandment's warning not to make an idol (Exodus 20:4). Rather, John repeatedly refers to God as "the one seated on the throne" (Revelation 4:9, 10; 5:1, 7, 13; see also 4:2, 3), highlighting God's majestic power to reign over the world. As the King of kings and Lord of lords, God is in a position to receive honor and worship.

To remind us of God's eternal nature, John also repeatedly calls God one "who is and was and is coming" (Revelation 1:4, 8; 4:8) and "who lives forever and ever" (4:9, 10)—this is an echo of the divine name that God revealed to Moses in Exodus 3:14, "I Am Who I Am" (or "I Will Be Who I Will Be"). Human life is limited in time; but the eternal God exists before, during, and after time. This sets up a very clear contrast with the Roman emperor. If the emperor conquers the world with a fearsome army, the almighty God who commands the angels and heavenly hosts is much more powerful. If the emperor terrifies people with violence and killing, the eternal God loves us and promises us a life of joy and peace even beyond death.

As the elders declare, all things in the world are created by God and exist by God's will; so God is worthy to receive glory and honor and power from the whole creation. God holds the scroll in which is written what will happen in the future (Revelation 5:1). This suggests that God is not only the Creator of the world, but the Lord of history. Because of this, it is right to worship God alone, as the first commandment requires (Exodus 20:3). Nothing else, including emperors or other idols, can demand allegiance or worship from us.

Christ the Lamb

The vision of the heavenly worship in Revelation 5 also reveals much about Christ. When John weeps over the thought that no one in the universe is worthy to open the scroll, an elder consoles him by saying that

Christ can do it because he is "the Lion of the tribe of Judah, the Root of David, [and] has emerged victorious" (Revelation 5:5). Both "Judah is a lion's cub" and "A shoot will grow up from the stump of Jesse" are Old Testament allusions to the Messiah, symbolizing his royal majesty and supremacy (Genesis 49:9; Isaiah 11:1). Christ (which means Messiah) has emerged victorious because he has defeated sin and death to redeem the world, doing so through the cross and resurrection. The Lion of Judah now stands between the throne and the living creatures as a Lamb that seems to have been slain (Revelation 5:6).

The Greek word used for "Lamb" is *arnion*, not the usual *amnos*. *Arnion* is the diminutive form, making the contrast between the Lion and the Lamb even starker. The humble little lamb is given a distinctive place of honor next to the throne of God because he has been slain for our sake. The scar of the cross has turned into a badge of triumph, and his fidelity and sacrifice prove that he is truly worthy to open the scroll. This theme is declared in the "new song" of praise that the living creatures and the elders are singing (Revelation 5:9) and is repeated in the thunderous chorus of the millions of angels (5:11-12).

Like almighty God, Christ the slain Lamb receives worship from the living creatures and the elders, prayers from the saints, songs of praise from the angels, and adoration from all creatures in heaven and on earth and under the earth and in the sea (Revelation 5:8-13). He is praised for purchasing for God, by his blood, "persons from every tribe, language, people, and nation" (5:9). The result is that everyone in the heavenly court worships Christ, side by side with God, with joyful songs of praise, saying,

> Blessing, honor, glory, and power belong
> to the one seated on the throne
> and to the Lamb
> forever and ever. (5:13)

Jesus, the Lamb of God

The term "Lamb of God" appears first in the Gospel of John, when John the Baptist sees Jesus coming toward him and says, "Look! The Lamb of God who takes away the sin of the world!" (1:29). As the Lamb of God, Jesus offers his blood on the cross as a perfect sacrificial offering, one that brings forgiveness and new life to all who believe. In Revelation, John says that he "saw a Lamb, standing as if it had been slain" (5:6), and hears the creatures of the heavenly court sing,

> You were slain,
> and by your blood you purchased for God
> persons from every tribe, language, people, and nation.
>
> (5:9)

The Latin term for Lamb of God is *Agnus Dei*, which has been used widely in Christian music.

Believers

In the worship of Christ the slaughtered Lamb, the new song of the living creatures and the elders reminds us that all believers have been purchased for God by Christ with the costly price of his blood. This redemption makes us "a kingdom and priests" to God (Revelation 5:10a). We are a kingdom that is in this world but not of the world, living a new way of life that follows the guidance of our Lord God rather than the drifting winds of culture. We are also priests of a holy God, devoted to worshiping God and reconciling people to God.

The new song goes on to promise that believers "will reign on earth" (Revelation 5:10). With God and Christ, believers are given the status and honor to reign with power to conquer sin, overcome evil, and live holy lives. This message was especially encouraging to John and the seven churches, forced by the agents of the imperial cult to violate the first commandment and pressured by local authorities to follow pagan customs and practices. For Christians today, the new song can help to renew our role, mission, and witness as God's holy and royal people in a challenging culture of disbelief.

So what is the proper way to worship God? As we follow John's description of the heavenly worship, we can identify with the twenty-four elders who represent the people of God. At the cue of the four living creatures surrounding the throne of God, they fall before God with the utmost humility (Revelation 4:10a), throw down their crowns before the throne to honor God's lordship over them (4:10c), and praise God with joyful thanks for the creation of "all things" (4:11). The elders also fall before Christ (5:8) and praise him with a new song, in thanks for his redemption of the world and his creation of a kingdom and priests of God (5:9-10). We can also identify with every creature in the universe, exuberant in their praise of God and Christ (5:13). In every time and place, praise-filled worship is a proper offering to our God and to the Lamb, the ones who have created, redeemed, and renewed us.

Like the overture in an opera, the vision of heavenly worship in Revelation 4–5 sums up who God and Christ are and what God and Christ are doing in the world. It prepares us to understand the divine drama of the events to come, reported in the visions of Revelation 6–22. This vision of heaven also suggests what faithful believers should do on earth, even while facing temptations and hardship—namely, praise and worship. As we offer songs of praise in unison with all the saints in heaven and on earth, the Holy Spirit will open our eyes to see the beauty of the world, the wonder of life, and the mystery of love. We will deepen our confidence in God's care and control and put more trust in Christ our Savior, even as we labor and suffer in this world. We will come to understand that God and Christ are continuing the work of creation, redemption, and renewal, as we sing the words of Charles Wesley, from his hymn "Love Divine, All Loves Excelling":

> Finish then thy new creation;
> pure and spotless let us be.
> Let us see thy great salvation
> perfectly restored in thee;
> changed from glory into glory,

till in heaven we take our place,
till we cast our crowns before thee,
lost in wonder, love, and praise.[1]

Live the Story

John's vision of heavenly worship takes place while the seven churches are enduring hardship in a culture of disbelief. He hears songs of praise that focus on God's creation and Christ's redemption and sees the sealed scroll with God's plan, which will be opened by Christ.

How do you picture yourself participating in the song of the elders and the angels, even while you are fighting the temptations and hardships of this world? Do you see a sign that our Creator God is more powerful than the evil of this world? Where is the evidence that the Lamb who was slain has begun his reign? Can you find a crack in the door to heaven, allowing you to see the scroll that will be opened by Christ? What will enable you to cast your crown before God and join all creation in wonder, love, and praise?

Worship is always a good place to begin. Remember that it was prayerful worship on the island of Patmos that enabled John to receive Jesus' messages "on the Lord's day" (Revelation 1:10). It was praise-filled worship in the heavenly court that prepared him to understand the messages that would follow. Once our spiritual eyes have a glimpse of the majesty of the God who created the world, we will be able to put everything in the world in perspective. Nothing is so big that God cannot take hold of it, and nothing is too small for God to care about. As Paul puts it, "Nothing can separate us from God's love in Christ Jesus our Lord" (Romans 8:38).

So what steps will you take this week to make some room for praise?

1. From "Love Divine, All Loves Excelling," in *The United Methodist Hymnal* (Copyright © 1989 by The United Methodist Publishing House); 384.

Victory Belongs to God

Revelation 6–11

Claim Your Story

Turn on the television or computer, and you are bombarded by live broadcasts of news events happening around the globe. The images are hard to forget: American soldiers patrolling the dangerous and rugged terrain of Afghanistan, Japanese people being pulled from the rubble of a massive earthquake, and Egyptians protesting in Cairo's Tahrir Square for democracy, or similar scenes

Broadcasts of natural disasters, such as hurricanes, blizzards, and earthquakes, are particularly frightening and humbling. We know that nature has certain laws, and some natural disasters are necessary to maintain the equilibrium of the ecosystem. Human behavior has an effect as well, as our exploitation of the environment degrades the land, fouls the water, and pollutes the air in ways that increase global warming. But when we witness the destructive force of cataclysmic events, we cannot help but wonder if there is anything mightier than the raw power of nature.

When lives are lost in natural disasters, we long for a sign of God's healing presence. When houses are washed away by hurricanes or leveled by earthquakes, we want to see evidence that there is a power greater than all these troubles. When our own life is a disaster, we have to ask, "Who will come to the rescue?"

Enter the Bible Story

John has just witnessed the solemn and splendid worship of God and the Lamb in the heavenly throne room. His gaze is fixed on the Lamb who is about to open the scroll. A secret plan of God is hidden there, but what can it be? We can feel the suspense and intense expectation.

As Christ the Lamb opens the seven seals one by one, John is stunned to see a series of visions of destruction, connected to four riders on horses and seven angels blowing trumpets. Heavenly voices make thunderous announcements, disclosing what will happen to the world. We are curious about what the visions and announcements might mean to John and his church. More importantly, we wonder, "What do they say to us today?"

The seven seals indicate that God's secret plan is important and needs to be safeguarded. Only one who is authorized can reveal the secret to the world. Suddenly, neither angels nor humans have to wait any longer because Christ the slaughtered Lamb has proved himself worthy to open the seals and reveal God's secret to John and to us (Revelation 5:9, 12). As John the Gospel writer said,

No one has ever seen God.
God the only Son,
who is at the Father's side,
has made God known. (John 1:18)

The Lamb of God who takes away the sin of the world by shedding his blood on the cross has been raised from the dead, exalted to the right hand of God, and given the authority to reveal God's plan for the world (compare Matthew 28:18; Philippians 2:5-11).

Jesus Christ is the trustworthy revealer of God's secret. Opening the seals shows that God has begun to take action to implement the divine plan, making Jesus Christ a potent agent of God's unfolding work in history. Christians can be confident that they are following a divine Savior, one in whom they can put their trust and hope.

Opening the Seals

When the first four seals are opened, riders on horses appear. They are sometimes called "The Four Horsemen of the Apocalypse." Sadly, these riders represent all too well the reality of horrific destruction in the world, both in John's time and in ours. Life is full of suffering and affliction, and there is little peace or justice to be found.

About the Scripture

The Four Horsemen of the Apocalypse

The Horsemen	Equipment	Significance
Rider on a white horse (6:2)	Carried a bow and was given a crown	Represents the war of conquest that seeks victories
Rider on a fiery red horse (6:4)	Given a large sword to take peace from the earth	Represents the rage of domination that instigates people to kill each other
Rider on a black horse (6:5)	Held a balance for weighing in the marketplace	Represents the greed of commerce that monopolizes and cheats
Rider named "Death" on a pale green horse (6:8)	Accompanied by Grave	Given authority over a fourth of the earth, to kill by sword, famine, disease, and the wild animals of the earth

Notice the many verbs used in the passive voice, for example, "Its rider was allowed to take peace from the earth" (Revelation 6:4). These riders were given permission by God to do what they did. The point of the "divine passive" is to communicate that almighty God remains firmly in control despite the presence of many destructive forces. But this raises a serious question: Why would a merciful God allow these destructive forces to afflict the innocent?

The very same question is raised by the souls of the martyrs buried under the altar, as the fifth seal is opened. "Holy and true Master, how long will you wait before you pass judgment? How long before you require justice for our blood, which was shed by those who live on earth?" (Revelation 6:10-11). The lamentation of the faithful martyrs raises a question of "theodicy" (justice of God), one that the psalmists frequently posed in the Old Testament (Psalms 13:1-2; 35:17; 94:3-4; 119:84). It makes us wonder, "If the almighty God who created the world is in control of history, why should the innocent faithful suffer from the destruction of war, rage, greed, and death? Why does a merciful God not stop evil, sin, and destruction? Why does a God of justice allow the wicked to go free without punishment?"

These questions continue to resonate deeply with us today. No one likes suffering and injustice. We often understand justice in terms of lex talionis (equity between crime and punishment), and we want justice to be swift. But Revelation reports that the faithful martyrs are told to rest a little longer, "until their fellow servants and brothers and sisters—who were about to be killed as they were—were finished" (6:11). It seems unfair to us that martyrs have to wait longer for justice and that additional believers will have to die. We want God's plan to include much swifter justice.

The opening of the sixth seal sheds some light on these upsetting questions. A great earthquake shakes the world so violently that nature is turned upside down. Suddenly, the sun, moon, stars, and sky—the constant elements of nature—lose their places and functions. All humans, from kings to slaves, are stricken with panic and frantically seek cover in caves because they know that the great day of the wrath of God and the Lamb has come; "and who is able to stand?" (Revelation 6:17). With images of the Final Judgment (Isaiah 13:9; Ezekiel 31:15; Malachi 4:1; Mark 13:24-27), this vision reassures us that the almighty God will render justice in the most fearful fashion. Divine judgment may seem delayed, but it is sure and awesome. When the wrath of God comes, no one can escape.

Gathering of the Faithful

After the opening of the sixth seal, an angel from the east, holding the seal of the living God, commands four other angels not to damage the earth and sea "until we have put a seal on the foreheads of those who serve our God" (Revelation 7:3). This reminds us of the story of the Passover, in which the Lord passed over the Hebrews who lived in houses marked with lamb's blood and struck the Egyptians with plagues (Exodus 12:13, 23). God is always mindful of the faithful and will protect them.

Then John sees a huge rally. All the faithful servants of God are gathered together in 2 groups. One group has 144,000 persons from the 12 tribes of Israel; and the other has an unnumbered multitude of believers from every nation, tribe, people, and language. They wear white robes and hold palm branches, symbols of purity and peace, singing loud praises:

> Victory belongs to our God
> who sits on the throne
> and to the Lamb. (Revelation 7:10)

Like the slaughtered Lamb, the faithful servants of God are pure and peaceful in character and behavior, giving them the ability to overcome evil and win final victory.

To encourage John and his readers, an angel points out that these faithful witnesses of God have survived great hardship. Their robes have been made white in the Lamb's blood, their purity has been proved by suffering, and their peace has been tested by hostile attacks. As a result, the Lamb will shepherd them; and God will wipe away their tears. The message for us is that God does not forget the faithful but shelters them forever (Revelation 7:13-17). This is how God renders justice and rewards the faithful.

Finally, the Lamb opens the seventh seal; and a long silence fills the heavens (Revelation 8:1). Silence is a sign of deep reverence and intense listening and often precedes an appearance of God in the Old Testament (Job 4:16; Zephaniah 1:7). So it is appropriate for all living things in heaven and on earth to keep silence before the great secret plan of God in the scroll is declared. The silence is finally broken by the grand sound of seven trumpets, fitting for the announcement of a royal edict and divine message.

Across the Testaments

Old Testament Images in Revelation's Gathering of the Faithful

Sealing of the faithful	Exodus 12:13 "The blood will be your sign on the houses where you live. Whenever I see the blood, I'll pass over you. No plague will destroy you when I strike the land of Egypt."	Revelation 7:3 "Don't damage the earth, the sea, or the trees until we have put a seal on the foreheads of those who serve our God."
Palm branches	Leviticus 23:40 "On the first day you must take fruit from majestic trees, palm branches, branches of leafy trees, and willows of the streams, and rejoice before the LORD your God for seven days."	Revelation 7:9 "They wore white robes and held palm branches in their hands."
Silence in God's presence	Zephaniah 1:7 "Hush before the LORD God, / for the day of the LORD is near!"	Revelation 8:1 "Then, when the Lamb opened the seventh seal, there was silence in heaven for about half an hour."

Seven Trumpets Blown

The seven trumpets introduce divine judgments that remind us of the ten plagues in Egypt (Exodus 7–12), but they are cosmic in scope. When the first four trumpets are blown, the natural world is shattered and becomes inhabitable. A third of the earth is burned up; a third of the sea becomes blood; a third of the river becomes bitter; and a third of the sun, moon, and stars become dark.

As terrifying as this environmental catastrophe is, an eagle declares that the last three trumpets will bring even more unbearable horrors to those who live on earth. Indeed, at the blowing of the fifth trumpet, a fallen star opens the shaft of the abyss to release a swarm of locusts. These iron-clad flying locusts are led by a mythical figure, Abaddon (in Hebrew) or Apollyon (in Greek), and look like a battalion of fighting machines (Revelation 9:11). Notice that they are allowed to hurt only those people who do not have the seal of God on their foreheads, and they are not to take lives (9:4-5). God the Creator alone has the power to give and take life.

At the blowing of the sixth trumpet, four angels formerly bound at the River Euphrates are released; and they kill a third of humankind (Revelation 9:15). Despite this massacre, the rest of humankind remains stubborn, refusing to change their hearts and behaviors (9:20-21). At that moment, a mighty angel descends from heaven with an open scroll and announces, "When the seventh angel blows his trumpet, God's mysterious purpose will be accomplished, fulfilling the good news he gave to his servants the prophets" (10:7). The believers are being urged to keep their faith alive.

Before the seventh trumpet is blown, John is ordered to eat the open scroll and "prophesy...about many peoples, nations, languages, and kings" (Revelation 10:9-11). The prophet Ezekiel was once commissioned to do the same (eat a scroll and prophesy); but he was sent specifically to the Israelites in exile, not to other peoples (Ezekiel 3:3-6). John is also given a measuring rod to measure God's temple, altar, and worshipers—but not the court outside the temple because it was given to the nations to trample for 42 months (compare Ezekiel 43:10-18). He is further told that 2 witnesses of God will prophesy for 1,260 days with miraculous powers. When they finish their mission, they will be killed by the beast coming up from the abyss; and their bodies will be left in the streets of Jerusalem, where Jesus Christ was crucified. After 3 1/2 days, they will be resurrected and go up to heaven in a cloud, witnessed by their enemies. An earthquake will kill 7,000 and terrify the rest (Revelation 11:1-14).

Finally, the seventh trumpet is blown; and the voices of heaven say,

> The kingdom of the world has become
> the kingdom of our Lord and his Christ,
> and he will reign forever and ever.
> (Revelation 11:15)

The elders also say,

> The nations were enraged, but your wrath came.
> The time came for the dead to be judged;
> The time came to reward your servants,
>> the prophets and saints,
>> and those who fear your name, both small and great,
>> and to destroy those who destroy the earth.
>>> (Revelation 11:18)

At that moment, God's temple in heaven is opened; and the ark of the covenant appears in the temple.

The Meaning of the Throne and the Altar

In Revelation 4–5, John sees the throne in the middle of the heavenly court, around which circles of elders and angels worship God and the Lamb without ceasing. In Revelation 6–11, he sees an altar at the center of the visions that reveal what will happen to the world. The throne symbolizes divine authority, while the altar is a sign of human sacrifice.

Under the altar are the souls of the martyrs, slaughtered on account of the word of God and their faithful witness (Revelation 6:9). In the temple service, the altar of sacrifice stands at the center of the holy space and is the heart of the acts of communication and reconciliation. There, worshipers offer their very best gifts to God, along with their thanks, regrets, and pleas. There, God meets the faithful and grants them divine blessings, pardons, and promises. Of all the gifts that can be given by humans, the sacrifices of the martyrs are most precious to God.

Why, then, does God want the martyrs to "rest a little longer" until more of their fellow servants and brothers and sisters are also martyred (Revelation 6:11)? It is hard for us to understand why God does not save the martyrs immediately and bring an end to the hardships that continue to afflict his faithful people. We ask many of the same questions when good people suffer today as a result of human violence or natural disasters.

One answer comes from 2 Peter 3:9, which says, "The Lord isn't slow to keep his promise, as some think of slowness, but he is patient toward you, not wanting anyone to perish but all to change their hearts and lives." Peter believes that God is giving people time to prepare for the "great day of...wrath" mentioned in Revelation 6:17, the day on which a final reckoning will take place and everybody will have to give an account before God and the Lamb. It is out of patience that God allows more time for people to make the right choice, even if this time includes hardship for people of faith.

God's Final Victory

The visions of Revelation 6–11 show that the world will undergo numerous disasters and human hardships before God's ultimate plan is fulfilled. Much of the earth will be destroyed and many human lives will be lost before the dawn of the new creation. Even faithful martyrs will suffer a bit longer, but this delay in the completion of God's plan will allow others to repent and come to God. Revelation's visions also assure us that faithful people will be gathered from all over the world and given eternal glory in the presence of God. God and the Lamb will have the final victory, and people of faith will join the heavenly hosts in joyful praise and worship.

Live the Story

When we face daunting challenges and painful hardships, it is frustrating to be told, "You have to endure it." We want to be assured that we can overcome the challenge and eliminate the hardship! A message of endurance is not what we want to hear.

But Revelation challenges us to be steadfast in our faith and to believe that

> victory belongs to our God
> who sits on the throne,
> and to the Lamb. (7:10)

Endurance becomes possible only when we gain the perspective of heaven and discover that God is in control. If we can see the final and glorious victory beyond the battles, we will be strengthened to fight on.

Continue to lift your concerns to God in prayer because even in times of injustice and destruction, God hears the cries of the faithful. In a moment of silence, imagine yourself standing among the faithful in heaven; and notice that God has already begun to reclaim the world for a new creation, while laying plans to gather the righteous for eternal blessings. Human evil and natural disasters may seem to be getting worse by the day, but these are only temporary; and they are allowed by God. Look at the world from a heavenly perspective, and know that God and the Lamb will lead you through your troubles to a final victory.

The Endurance of the Saints

Revelation 12–14

Claim Your Story

In The Chronicles of Narnia, C.S. Lewis created a fantasy world to teach lessons about the Christian faith. Narnia is a land full of obstacles and opportunities, battles and betrayals, dangers and deaths—just like our own land. The future of Narnia is balanced on the lives of four bewildered children, boys and girls who must find inside themselves the courage and the faith to work alongside Aslan the lion.

Aslan is one of the best fictional representations of Jesus Christ. Although good and loving, Aslan is *not* a tame lion. He represents "the Lion of the tribe of Judah" (Revelation 5:5), a powerful beast who calls on his followers to be brave and trusting as they face challenges together.

Both the visions of Revelation and the land of Narnia contain strange creatures, good and evil, who fight to control the future of the world. Evil is real in these accounts and does fierce battle with goodness. In the middle of your own struggles, will you summon the courage to take a strong stand with God? When weakened by doubt and fear, will you find enough faith to resist the lure of the beasts that want to lead you astray?

Enter the Bible Story

After the last of the seven trumpets is blown, John looks to heaven and sees the first in a series of signs that are as dramatic and thrilling as anything in The Chronicles of Narnia. He spots a woman "clothed with the sun, with the moon under her feet and a crown of twelve stars on her head" (Revelation 12:1). She is pregnant and cries out in labor pains—like people in a time of judgment. In his letter to the Romans, Paul uses a similar image of childbirth to describe the painful birth of God's new creation (8:22-23).

Satan, Mother, and Child

Then a great fiery dragon appears, "with seven heads and ten horns, and seven royal crowns on his heads" (Revelation 12:3). The dragon is Satan, and he stands in front of the woman to devour her child when she gives birth. But a divine power intervenes, snatching the child up to God as soon as he is born. The child is "a son, a male child who is to rule all the nations with an iron rod" (12:5).

The woman flees into the desert, where God has prepared a place for her. There she is taken care of for 1,260 days (Revelation 12:6). The desert is the place where Jesus was tempted, but he was also cared for there by angels (Matthew 4:11). This woman's escape echoes the flight of Jesus and his parents to Egypt (Matthew 2:13), as well as Ishmael and Hagar's time in the desert (Genesis 21:9-21). We can sense danger, insecurity, and vulnerability in all these stories—conditions that are reflected in our own lives today. But the good news is that God provides for those who maintain their faith and trust.

Fighting in Heaven

Then a war breaks out in heaven, in which Michael and his angels fight the dragon. Introduced in the Book of Daniel as "the great leader" (or "the great prince" [NRSV]) and protector of God's people (Daniel 12:1), he is an archangel who "argued with the devil" (Jude 9). The dragon and his angels respond fiercely, but they cannot overcome the powers of good; so they lose their place in heaven.

John describes the great dragon as the "old snake, who is called the devil and Satan, the deceiver of the whole world," and announces that he is thrown down to the earth, along with his angels (Revelation 12:9). This heavenly battle reminds us that intense struggles are not limited to life on earth, at least until God's new heaven and new earth are firmly in place. At this point it appears that the ejection of Satan from heaven is going to create trouble for the inhabitants of the earth.

Across the Testaments

Personifications of Evil in the Old and New Testaments

Satan has a long and evolving history through the Bible. In Genesis, we meet the snake, who is not explicitly identified as Satan but rather as "the most intelligent of all the wild animals that the Lord God had made" (3:1). Then in Job, Satan is called the "Adversary" (1:6) and functions as the prosecuting attorney in the trial of the righteous man Job, challenging God to "stretch out your hand and strike all he has" (1:11). The New Testament begins with the devil tempting Jesus after his baptism; and Jesus concludes this trial by saying, "Go away, Satan" (Matthew 4:10). In Second Corinthians, Paul warns his followers of the devil's power to deceive when he says, "Even Satan disguises himself as an angel of light" (11:14). Finally, in Revelation, the devil is introduced as the "old snake, who is called the devil and Satan, the deceiver of the whole world" (12:9), and is later defeated and "thrown into the lake of fire and sulfur" (20:10).

The throwing down of Satan has an immediate benefit for those who believe. John hears a voice from heaven say,

> Now the salvation and power and kingdom of our God,
>   and the authority of his Christ have come.
> For the accuser of our brothers and sisters,
>   who accuses them day and night before our God,
>   has been thrown down. (Revelation 12:10)

Satan had continued to act as a prosecuting attorney, much as he did in the Book of Job, making accusations about people to God. But now Satan has been thrown out of court.

According to the voice from heaven, believers have gained victory over Satan by the blood of the Lamb, the word of their testimony, and their willingness to be martyred (Revelation 12:11). But the winning of this one battle does not mean that the fighting is over. John realizes that rejoicing in heaven is going to be balanced by horror on earth because the devil has come down "with great rage, / for he knows that he only has a short time" (12:12).

Danger on Earth

As the fighting moves from heaven to earth, the dragon chases the woman who had given birth to the child. But the woman is offered two wings of a great eagle so that she can fly to her place in the desert (Revelation 12:13-14). She is completely dependent on God, and through her faith she discovers that the promise of Isaiah is true:

> Those who hope in the LORD will renew their strength;
>   they will fly up on wings like eagles;
> they will run and not be tired;
>   they will walk and not be weary. (40:31)

Faith and hope give her a lift to a better place, and what is true for her is true for us as well.

Satan the dragon is persistent, however. He pours a river of water after the woman to sweep her away, but the earth helps the woman by opening its mouth and swallowing the river (Revelation 12:15-16). In many places in the Bible, water is a sign of chaos—from the first day of Creation when "God's wind swept over the waters" (Genesis 1:2) to the day on the Sea of Galilee when Jesus forced the wind and the sea to obey him (Mark 4:41). In Revelation, God's good earth takes action to swallow the river of chaos and protect the vulnerable woman.

Furious, Satan stomps off to make war on the rest of the woman's children, all those who "keep God's commandments and hold firmly to the witness of Jesus" (Revelation 12:17). It appears that the fighting between Satan and God's people is going to escalate, as the dragon stands on the seashore and looks for an ally to emerge from the sea.

The Beast From the Sea

Suddenly, John sees a beast coming up out of the sea, which like the river is a symbol of watery chaos. The beast resembles Satan with its 10 horns, 7 heads, and royal crowns; and "on its heads were blasphemous names" (Revelation 13:1). These blasphemous names are in stark contrast to the name of God and the Lamb, which will appear on the foreheads of the 144,000 believers (14:1) and on the foreheads of the servants of God (22:4).

The dragon gives this beast "his power, throne, and great authority" (Revelation 13:2); and confusion is created by the fact that one of the beast's heads appears to have been killed, like the Lamb of God "standing as if it had been slain" (5:6). John reports that "the whole earth" is amazed and follows the beast and worships Satan the dragon (13:3-4). People stand in awe of the raw power of this beast from the sea, unable to conceive of any force that could defeat it.

The beast speaks "boastful and blasphemous things"—insulting God, God's name, God's dwelling place, and God's people in heaven (Revelation 13:5-6). John says that the beast "was given authority to act for forty-two months" (13:5), suggesting by the use of the passive "was given authority" that it was given permission by God to do what it did, but for a limited time. As with the four horsemen in Revelation 6, this use of the "divine passive" communicates that God is in control despite the presence of destructive forces.

The beast from the sea is allowed to make war on the saints and to gain victory and is "given authority over every tribe, people, language, and nation" (Revelation 13:7). This is a horrifying reversal of the new song of Revelation 5, in which the heavenly creatures praise Christ the Lamb for purchasing with his blood "persons from every tribe, language, people, and nation" (5:9).

All who live on earth worship the beast, except for those whose names have been written "in the Scroll of Life of the Lamb who was slain" (Revelation 13:8). John does not reveal the names written in the scroll but issues a call for "endurance and faithfulness on the part of the saints" (13:10). And then the vision goes from bad to worse.

The Beast From the Land

John sees another beast coming up from the earth, and this creature compounds the damage being done by the first beast. With horns like a lamb and the voice of a dragon, it exercises all of the authority of the first beast and forces all people of the earth to "worship the first beast, whose fatal wound was healed" (Revelation 13:11-12). John may have been warning his followers about the high priest of the imperial cult, who demanded that people bow down to the Roman emperor as "Lord and God."

For Christians, any worship of a human or a human image is idolatry; so John is deeply concerned when the beast from the land tells the people of the earth to make "an image for the beast who had been wounded by the sword and yet came to life again" (Revelation 13:14). The beast who "had been wounded" may have been the Emperor Nero, who was assassinated in A.D. 68 but was rumored to have survived and fled. For decades people talked of his possible return as emperor.

Anyone who does not worship the beast's image is put to death (Revelation 13:15)—the ultimate punishment for those who do not conform to the expectations of the imperial cult. The beast also forces everyone to have a mark put on their right hand or their forehead, and people are prohibited from purchasing or selling anything until they have the mark of the beast (13:16-17). Those who honor the emperor have complete freedom in the marketplace, while those who refuse to participate in the imperial cult are subjected to economic and social consequences.

"This calls for wisdom," says John. "Let the one who understands calculate the beast's number, for it's a human being's number. Its number is six hundred and sixty-six" (Revelation 13:18). Numerous interpretations have been given to this number. In Hebrew, the numerical value of the name Nero Caesar is 666. In Greek, the numerical value of the name Jesus is 888, so 666 is a contrasting and clearly lower number. If 7 is the number of perfection, as it is often used in the Book of Revelation, then the number 6 is imperfection—tripled! However the number is interpreted, it reminds us of the power and danger of idolatry, in both the first century and today.

About the Christian Faith

The Identity of the Beast Whose Number Is 666

According to . . .	The Beast is . . .
The first-century church of Ephesus	The high priest of the imperial cult
Some medieval Christians, particularly Pope Innocent III	The Islamic prophet Mohammed
Some Protestant Reformers, including Martin Luther	The Papacy
Some members of the Seventh-Day Adventist Church (in the 1800s)	The United States of America
English occultist Aleister Crowley (1875–1947)	Himself

The Lamb and the 144,000

The scene changes; and now John sees the Lamb, standing on Mount Zion—the place associated with the presence of God. With the Lamb are 144,000 righteous people who have the name of the Lamb and God "written on their foreheads" (14:1), in stark contrast to the people in the previous chapter who bear the mark of the beast (13:16).

John hears a sound from heaven that is like the sound of rushing water and loud thunder, like that of harpists playing their harps. Just as in Revelation 5, the 4 living creatures and elders sing a song in front of the throne; but this time no one can learn the song except the 144,000 people who have been purchased for God from the earth (Revelation 14:2-3).

And what is so special about these people? John tells us that they are sexually pure (unlike participants in pagan cults), they follow the Lamb, they speak the truth, and they are morally blameless. The 144,000 are not the sum total of the elect but are described as "firstfruits for God and the Lamb," meaning that they are the first fruits of the great harvest of righteous people to come (Revelation 14:4-5). By following their example, we can look forward to joining them in heaven.

Messages From Three Angels

Then John sees three angels. One commands people to "fear God and give him glory, for the hour of his judgment has come" (Revelation 14:7). The second announces that Babylon is fallen (14:8). The third gives the warning, "If any worship the beast and its image, and receive a mark on their foreheads or their hands, they themselves will also drink the wine of God's passionate anger, poured full strength into the cup of his wrath"— they will experience eternal punishment (14:9-11). The contrast is now perfectly clear between the fate of those who bear the name of the Lamb and God and those who have the mark of the beast.

So how should we respond? We should fear God and give him glory rather than bowing down to the political, military, or economic idols of this world. We should know that our worship of creatures instead of the Creator will have dire consequences. Finally, we should practice "the endurance of the saints, who keep God's commandments and keep faith with Jesus" (Revelation 14:12). The marching orders of the saints of God are worship, endurance, commandment-keeping, and faith.

Then a voice from heaven commands John to write the words, "Favored are the dead who die in the Lord from now on." And the Spirit of God says, "Yes, so they can rest from their labors, because their deeds follow them" (Revelation 14:13). John is asked to make a note of these words of promise and encouragement so that the suffering Christians of the earth will know that their righteous deeds will never be forgotten.

Two Harvests

John sees a white cloud; and on it is someone who looks like "the Human One" ("the Son of Man" [NRSV]), with "a golden crown on his head and sharp sickle in his hand" (Revelation 14:14). An angel says to him, "Use your sickle to reap the harvest" (14:15). So the Human One swings his sickle, and the earth is harvested (14:16). This seems to be a harvest of good fruit, perhaps one that adds to the "firstfruits" of Revelation 14:4.

Then comes another angel with a sharp sickle, to cut the clusters in the vineyard of the earth. The angel swings his sickle and puts what he reaps into "the great winepress of God's passionate anger." Bad fruit is crushed until blood comes out of the winepress "as high as the horses' bridles" (Revelation 14:17-20).

Centuries after John's vision, this image appears in the first line of "The Battle Hymn of the Republic":

> Mine eyes have seen the glory of
> the coming of the Lord;
> he is trampling out the vintage
> where the grapes of wrath are stored.[1]

The harvest of redemption is followed by the harvest of judgment.

Live the Story

We live in the real world, not a fantasy land like Narnia. And yet the tales of strange creatures in unusual places can teach valuable lessons about how to endure the struggles of life today. Both Aslan the lion and Jesus the Lamb have much the same message: Although evil is real and battles goodness, it cannot triumph. In the end, God and those who stand with God will win.

When you face danger and feel vulnerable, remember the story of the woman in Revelation: God protects and provides for those who maintain their faith and trust. When the destructive forces of hostile powers seem overwhelming, remember the tale of the beast from the sea: The way to survive is to practice endurance and faithfulness. When you are tempted to bow down to unjust earthly rulers who promise you power or success, remember the vision of the beast from the earth: You do not want to gain the whole world and lose your soul.

During the week to come, reflect on these powerful images when you face difficulties that threaten to overwhelm you. They vividly illustrate the truth that God is on your side, giving you the ability to practice the endurance of the saints.

1. From "Mine Eyes Have Seen the Glory (The Battle Hymn of the Republic)," in *The United Methodist Hymnal* (Copyright © 1989 by The United Methodist Publishing House); 717.

5

God's Judgments Are Just

Revelation 15–16

Claim Your Story

The years 2011 through 2015 mark the 150th anniversary of the Civil War, which historian James H. Moorhead calls an "American apocalypse." The war was a kind of apocalyptic struggle, with the Northern armies seeing themselves as fighting for the Lord on the chaotic field of Armageddon. The words of "The Battle Hymn of the Republic" proclaimed that the freeing of the slaves was holy work:

> In the beauty of the lilies
> Christ was born across the sea,
> with a glory in his bosom
> that transfigures you and me;
> as he died to make men holy,
> let us die to make men free,
> while God is marching on.[1]

An accurate understanding of an apocalyptic book such as Revelation requires that you see God's work from the perspective of an oppressed person—such as a slave during the Civil War. Otherwise, the wrath and the justice of God seem excessively harsh. But if you put yourself in the position of a slave in America or a Christian in the Roman Empire, then God's judgments make perfect sense.

Think of a situation in which you have suffered oppression—from individuals or institutions—and imagine how the wrath of God could be a welcome relief. From this perspective, times of chaos can be opportunities to witness God's justice and pursue a God-blessed course.

Enter the Bible Story

The harvest of judgment has been completed; and now the wrath of God is unleashed, revealing God's passion for justice. Revelation 15–16 shows that God cares for the suffering and the innocent and is determined to hold oppressors accountable. In the verses that follow, John is given visions of God's mighty power, holiness, and judgment—a judgment that is both just and horrifying.

Chapter 15 begins with John seeing another great and awe-inspiring sign in heaven: "There were seven angels with seven plagues—and these are the last, for with them God's anger is brought to an end. Then I saw what appeared to be a sea of glass mixed with fire. Those who gained victory over the beast, its image, and the number of its name were standing by the glass sea, holding harps from God" (Revelation 15:1-2). The sea of glass is similar to the sea in front of the throne in 4:6, except that this one is mixed with fire. Beside the sea are the martyrs of God (13:1-10), who have gained victory over the beast from the sea. They sing a song (15:3-4) that is a dramatic commentary on the acts of judgment that will be unleashed in the plagues that follow.

The Song of Moses and the Lamb

The martyrs sing the song of Moses, God's servant, and the song of the Lamb—a song of praise that God's justice has been done (Revelation 15:3-4). Their words are reminiscent of the song Moses sang after God's triumph over the Egyptians (Exodus 15:1-18) and the poem he recited at the end of his life, praising God for God's mighty acts through history (Deuteronomy 32:1-43). Because signs of God's power and justice did not end with Moses but continued with Jesus Christ, the song is also "of the Lamb" (Revelation 15:3). John senses that Jesus is a new Moses, leading his people out of captivity into a new and better land.

The song begins with praise for God's power, preparing John for the plagues that will come in Revelation 16: "Great and awe-inspiring are your works, / Lord God Almighty" (15:3a). The martyrs then sing of God's holiness, knowing that only God is just, true, and holy in an unholy world:

> Just and true are your ways,
> king of the nations.
> Who won't fear you, Lord, and glorify your name?
> For you alone are holy. (15:3b-4b)

The song concludes with the prediction that all will worship God when God's acts of justice are displayed: "All nations will come and fall down in worship before you, / for your acts of justice have been revealed" (15:4c).

The revelation of God's justice is always greeted with joy by faithful people. African Americans and others rejoiced when slavery was ended by the Civil War and then when segregation was overcome by the civil rights movement. Even today, we praise God whenever a tyrant is overthrown, a corrupt corporation is punished, or a bad law is repealed.

Plagues Against Pharaoh and Caesar

After this dramatic song, John looks and sees that the temple in heaven is opened. He describes it as "the tent of witness" (Revelation 15:5), which was the portable tabernacle or sanctuary for God that the Israelites carried with them through the wilderness (Exodus 25–27). The temple is opened; and seven angels with plagues come out of the temple, clothed in pure bright linen with "golden sashes around their waists" (15:6)—similar to the linen and sashes worn by Aaron and his sons, the priests of Israel (Exodus 39:27-29).

John sees one of the four living creatures (see Revelation 4:6b-7) give the seven angels seven golden bowls "full of the anger of the God who lives forever" (Revelation 15:7). The wrath of God is about to be released, bringing justice to the oppressed and punishment to the oppressors. John sees that the temple is filled "with smoke from God's glory and power" (15:8), as in Isaiah's vision of the divine throne room (Isaiah 6:1-4). No one can go into the temple until the seven plagues of the angels are brought to an end (15:8).

A strong connection is made in this chapter between Revelation and Exodus. Both books have a tent of witness, angels or priests in linen and sashes, and plagues that demonstrate God's wrath. In Exodus, God's anger is directed toward Pharaoh; and in Revelation, it is aimed at Caesar. Both leaders have oppressed God's people and need to be brought to justice.

Plagues of Sores and Blood

The plagues that come from the seven bowls remind us of what God did to the Egyptians as the Israelites were liberated. These supernatural acts are part of our sacred memory, reminding us that God is always at work to save the suffering and the innocent, while punishing their oppressors. It is no surprise that persecuted churches throughout history have loved Revelation.

John hears a loud voice from the temple say to the seven angels, "Go and pour out the seven bowls of God's anger on the earth" (Revelation 16:1). The first angel pours his bowl on the earth; and "a nasty and terrible sore" appears on the people "who had the beast's mark and worshipped its image" (16:2), like the sores that broke out on people and animals in Egypt (Exodus 9:10).

The second angel pours his bowl into the sea; and the sea turns into blood, killing every living thing in the sea. The third angel pours his bowl into rivers and springs, turning them into blood as well (Revelation 16:3-4). Both of these plagues connect to the time in Egypt when Moses raised the shepherd's rod, hit the water in the Nile, and turned it into blood (Exodus 7:20).

The Wrath of God in the Old and New Testaments

The Song of Moses	Exodus 15:1-3 "Then Moses and the Israelites sang this song to the LORD: I will sing to the LORD, for an overflowing victory! Horse and rider he threw into the sea! The LORD is my strength and my power; he has become my salvation. This is my God, whom I will praise, the God of my ancestors, whom I will acclaim. The LORD is a warrior; the LORD is his name."	Revelation 15:3-4 "They sing the song of Moses, God's servant, and the song of the Lamb, saying, / 'Great and awe-inspiring are your works, / Lord God Almighty. / Just and true are your ways, / king of the nations. / Who won't fear you, Lord, and glorify your name? / For you alone are holy. / All nations will come and fall down in worship before you, / for your acts of justice have been revealed.' "
Sores	Exodus 9:10 "Moses threw the ash up in the air, and it caused skin sores and blisters to break out on people and animals."	Revelation 16:2 "A nasty and terrible sore appeared on the people who had the beast's mark."
Rivers Turned to Blood	Exodus 7:20 "All the water in the Nile turned into blood."	Revelation 16:4 "The rivers and springs of water…turned into blood."
Darkness Covered the Kingdom	Exodus 10:22 "So Moses raised his hand toward the sky, and an intense darkness fell on the whole land of Egypt for three days."	Revelation 16:10 "Darkness covered its kingdom."
Frogs	Exodus 8:6 "So Aaron stretched out his hand over the waters of Egypt. The frogs crawled up and covered the land of Egypt."	Revelation 16:13 "I saw three unclean spirits, like frogs, come from the dragon's mouth, the beast's mouth, and the mouth of the false prophet."

Lightning, thunder, and hail	Exodus 9:23 "Then Moses raised his shepherd's rod toward the sky, and the LORD sent thunder and hail, and lightning struck the earth."	Revelation 16:18-21 "There were lightning strikes, voices, and thunder, and a great earthquake occurred.... Huge hailstones weighing about one hundred pounds came down from heaven on the people."

One of the angels, called "the angel of the waters" (Revelation 16:5), becomes a divine interpreter of these events. The angel says, "You are just, holy one, who is and was, / because you have given these judgments" (16:5). God is described as just and holy, and God's judgments are praised—similar to the language of the Song of Moses and the Lamb (15:3-4). This God is the one "who is and was" (16:5), clearly the same God of Exodus whose name is "I Am Who I Am" (Exodus 3:14).

The angel goes on to speak of divine vengeance: "They poured out the blood of saints and prophets, / and you have given them blood to drink. They deserve it!" (Revelation 16:6). In an act of divine retribution, water turns to blood in front of the oppressors because they have "poured out the blood of the saints and prophets" (16:6). They deserve to drink this blood because of their evil acts, insists the angel of the waters.

Then the altar offers its approval, saying, "Yes, Lord God Almighty, your judgments are true and just" (Revelation 16:7). God has answered the cry of the martyrs and avenged their deaths. When we turn to God for help in times of chaos, we can trust God to hear our cries and respond.

Plagues of Heat, Darkness, and Drought

John's attention shifts to the sky; and a fourth angel pours his bowl on the sun, and it is allowed (once again, the "divine passive" is used, as in Revelation 6 and 13) "to burn people with fire" (16:8). People are scorched by the intense heat, and they curse the name of God; but they do not "change their hearts and lives and give him glory" (16:9). They remain stubborn, just like Pharaoh (Exodus 7:13, 22; 8:15, 19, 32; 9:34).

The fifth angel dumps his bowl over the beast's throne; and darkness covers its kingdom, the Roman Empire—as when "an intense darkness fell on the whole land of Egypt" (Exodus 10:22). People bite their tongues because of their pain and curse God, but again they do not repent (Revelation 16:10-11). The oppressors in the Roman Empire are as stubborn as the pharaoh of Egypt; but unlike Pharaoh, their hearts are not made stubborn by God (Exodus 10:1). They have freedom to repent, which is something that John is calling all his readers to do.

Then the sixth angel pours his bowl on the great river Euphrates, causing its water to dry up (Revelation 16:12). John sees three unclean spirits, like frogs, come from the mouth of the dragon (Satan, see 12:9), the mouth of the beast (perhaps the Roman emperor, see 13:1-10), and the mouth of the false prophet (perhaps the high priest of the imperial cult, see 13:11-18; 19:20) (16:13). John says, "These are demonic spirits that do signs" (16:14), like the spirits that Paul warns Timothy about when he says, "In latter times some people will turn away from the faith" and "will pay attention to spirits that deceive and to the teaching of demons" (1 Timothy 4:1). John is encouraging his followers to remain faithful as they face ongoing persecution and temptation.

The particular mission of the froglike demonic spirits is to "go out to the kings of the whole world, to gather them for battle on the great day of God the Almighty" (Revelation 16:14). In Revelation 19, the beast and the kings of the earth will gather to make war on Christ and his armies (19:19). John reports that "the spirits gathered them at the place that is called in Hebrew, Harmagedon [or Armageddon]" (16:16), a place that was the site of several decisive battles in the history of Israel.

Notice, however, that no fighting takes place in Revelation 16:12-15. Although the demonic spirits gather the kings, war does not break out. The hostilities are delayed, perhaps to give people time to repent. Earlier, Christ had called the church in Sardis to repentance, saying, "So remember what you received and heard. Hold on to it and change your hearts and lives. If you don't wake up, I will come like a thief, and you won't know what time I will come upon you" (3:3). Jesus has come, not to condemn the world, but to save it; and here he gives people time to change their hearts and pursue a God-blessed course.

John seems to be alluding to this passage from the Sardis message when he includes a parenthetical statement in the middle of his description of the gathering of the kings for battle: "Look! I am coming like a thief! Favored are those who stay awake and clothed so that they don't go around naked and exposed to shame" (16:15). Jesus wants us all to be prepared for his coming instead of being obsessed with making predictions about future events such as the Battle of Armageddon.

About the Scripture

Armageddon

The word *Armageddon* appears only once in the New Testament, in Revelation 16:16, which says that demonic spirits will gather kings to do battle "at the place that is called in Hebrew, Harmagedon [or Armageddon]." Harmagedon means "Mountain of Meggido," the location of many critical battles in ancient times, about twenty-five miles from the Sea of Galilee. This reference to Armageddon in Revelation 16:12-16 suggests that there will be an epic battle on this site at the end of time, on the "great day of God the Almighty," although the warfare between God and Satan in Revelation 19 and 20 makes no mention of this location. The word has come to be applied to any number of catastrophically destructive battles (the First World War has been called an Armageddon) or societal disasters (Financial Armageddon).

A Plague of Lightning, Thunder, and Earthquake

Finally, the seventh angel empties his bowl into the air; and a loud voice comes out from the temple, from the throne, saying, "It is done!" (Revelation 16:17). In a powerful finale, there are lightning strikes, voices, thunder, and a great earthquake—the greatest in the history of humankind (16:18). The fury of God's wrath produces a truly chaotic and apocalyptic scene, one that is simultaneously a comfort to the oppressed and a warning to oppressors.

John says that the great city (Rome) splits into three parts, and the cities of the nations fall. The punishment of God is directed particularly on big cities because they are places of human wealth, power, and pride. God remembers Babylon the great—a code name for Rome—and gives her "the wine-cup of his furious anger" (Revelation 16:19). The divinely ordained earthquake delivers a devastating blow, one that causes cities to fall, islands to flee, and mountains to disappear (16:19, 20). Huge hailstones come down from heaven on the people (16:21), just as hail fell on the oppressive Egyptians (Exodus 9:23-24). The people curse God for the plague of hail because the plague is so terrible (16:21).

Live the Story

When we look to God for help, times of chaos can be opportunities to witness God's justice and pursue a God-blessed course. The promise of the seven plagues is that God has a passion to liberate the oppressed and rescue those who are innocent victims. When we speak of the wrath of God, we should always remember that anger is a part of God's divine justice.

Revelation teaches us that God answers the cries of his faithful people and saves them from destruction. When you feel that you are a victim of unjust people or institutions, know that God is on your side and will support you in the process of achieving justice. We also learn from Revelation that God is patient with us, giving us time to change our hearts and lives and pursue God's will and God's way. Times of chaos can be good opportunities to look inward and repent of the attitudes and actions that steer us away from God.

The seven plagues are a warning to us that we should not turn into oppressors because God punishes those who oppress the weak, the different, and the unpopular. It is not easy to see ourselves clearly—remember that slave owners during the Civil War thought that they were upstanding Christian men and women. In your quiet time this week, do some self-examination and ask yourself, *Whom do I look down on? Whom do I despise because of their differences? Whom do I ignore or fail to include? the immigrant? the child with special needs? the difficult neighbor?*

God is very judgmental of human power and pride. Pursuing a God-blessed course begins with seeing everyone as a potential saint or prophet.

1. From "Mine Eyes Have Seen the Glory (The Battle Hymn of the Republic)," in *The United Methodist Hymnal* (Copyright © 1989 by The United Methodist Publishing House); 717.

Loose and Extravagant Ways

Revelation 17–18

Claim Your Story

Dave Ramsey, the popular host of a radio show on financial topics, says, "We buy things we don't even need with money we don't even have to impress people we don't even know."[1] He is absolutely right. We Americans are attracted to large houses, luxury cars, and the latest electronics, which we purchase with jumbo mortgages, auto loans, and ever-increasing credit card debt.

Although we think that such material goods will make us happy, we quickly discover that the opposite is true. Luxury items do not provide lasting satisfaction, debt increases our anxiety, and the people we want to impress remain distant from us. No matter how much money we have, we always believe that just a little more will bring us happiness and security.

God knows the seductive power of worldly wealth—in the ancient world and today—which is why Revelation contains two chapters on the danger of materialism. In a Spirit-induced trance, John sees a vision of an attractive woman named Babylon, who represents the most harmful aspects of the global economy. Her way is tempting and attractive, but it leads to destruction. God's way is the path that leads to life.

The Dave Ramsey Show is promoted with the tagline, "It's about your life and your money."[2] The same could be said about these chapters of Revelation.

Enter the Bible Story

God's passion for justice is seen in the liberation of oppressed people, as well as in the judgment of unjust economic systems. At the time of Revelation, the city of Rome is a powerful center of commerce that has grown wealthy from the labor of people throughout the Empire. Although Rome seems invincible, John knows that worldly riches are transient and that societies built on exploitation will fall. He believes that God will bring the Empire down, in a collapse far more dramatic than the Great Recession of 2008 was for us in the United States.

The Woman Named Babylon and the Beast

One of the seven angels with the seven bowls calls for John, saying, "I will show you the judgment upon the great prostitute, who is seated on many waters. The kings of the earth have committed sexual immorality with her, and those who live on earth have become drunk with the wine of her whoring" (Revelation 17:1-2).

The woman is the city of Rome, and the kings are the leaders of Asia Minor who have sided with the Roman Empire in its vast economic enterprises. God knows the attraction of power and wealth and passes judgment on those who have been seduced by it. Rome is a "great prostitute," says the angel, a whore who has slept with kings and intoxicated others.

John is aware that the words of Jesus are correct: "You cannot serve God and wealth" (Matthew 6:24). The worship of God always competes with the worship of earthly riches—both in ancient Rome and in modern America. God's judgment on the great prostitute is a warning to us about the danger of materialism.

Then the angel leads John "in a Spirit-inspired trance to a desert" (Revelation 17:3)—just as he was "in a Spirit-inspired trance on the Lord's day" when Revelation began (1:10). In the desert, John sees a woman (the city of Rome) seated on a scarlet beast (the Roman Empire), which like the beast from the sea (13:1-10) has seven heads, ten horns, and is "covered with blasphemous names" (17:3). Peter also used "Babylon" as a code word for the city of Rome (17:5) when he wrote, "The fellow-elect church in Babylon greets you, and so does my son Mark" (1 Peter 5:13). The woman is dressed beautifully in clothing that is scarlet and purple (the most expensive color of the day), and she glitters with "gold and jewels and pearls" (Revelation 17:4). (For years, Christian women were steered away from dressing in the color red because of the association between scarlet and this evil woman.) In her hand is a "golden cup full of the vile and impure things that came from her activity as a prostitute" (17:4), referring to the unjust ways that she has gathered wealth from throughout the Empire, using military and economic pressure. The mysterious name written on her forehead points to the seductiveness of her style of commerce: "Babylon the great, the mother of prostitutes and the vile things of the earth" (17:5).

John knows that her wealth has come at a tragic human cost and says, "The woman was drunk on the blood of the saints and the blood of Jesus' witnesses" (Revelation 17:6). He is completely stunned when he sees this horrible persecutor of the saints of God.

Seven Hills and Seven Kings

"Why are you amazed?" the angel asks; and then he says to John, "I will tell you the mystery of the woman and the seven-headed, ten-horned beast that carries her" (Revelation 17:7). The angel explains, "The beast that you saw was and is not, and is about to come up out of the abyss and go to destruction" (17:8). He is describing Nero, the emperor who was expected to return to life and resume his leadership role (see the descriptions of the beasts in Chapter 4 of this study). Because of the danger of speaking openly about such matters, John says, "This calls for an understanding mind" (17:9).

Continuing this explanation, the angel points out, "The seven heads are seven mountains on which the woman is seated. They are also seven kings" (Revelation 17:9). The seven heads of the beast represent the seven hills of Rome and also the seven kings (emperors) of Rome—leaders who are considered to be divine by the imperial cult and problematic for Christians.

Across the Testaments

Babylon, From Old Testament to New

Site of Israel's exile	2 Kings 24:15 "Nebuchadnezzar exiled Jehoiachin to Babylon; he also exiled the queen mother, the king's wives, the officials, and the land's elite leaders from Jerusalem to Babylon."	Matthew 1:17 "So there were fourteen generations from Abraham to David, fourteen generations from David to the exile to Babylon, and fourteen generations from the exile to Babylon to the Christ."
Place of grief	Psalm 137:1 "Alongside Babylon's streams, / there we sat down, / crying because we remembered Zion."	Revelation 18:11 "The merchants of the earth will weep and mourn over [Babylon], for no one buys their cargoes anymore."
Object of curse	Psalm 137:8 "Daughter Babylon, you destroyer, / a blessing on the one who pays you back / the very deed you did to us!"	Revelation 16:19 "God remembered Babylon the great so that he gave her the wine cup of his furious anger."
Wealthy city, destined to fall	Isaiah 13:19 "Babylon, / a jewel among kingdoms, / the Chaldeans' splendor and pride, / will be like Sodom and Gomorrah, / destroyed by God."	Revelation 18:10 "Babylon, you great city, you powerful city! In a single hour your judgment has come."
Place of idols and demons	Jeremiah 50:2 "Babylon is captured; / Bel is shamed, / Marduk is panic-stricken. / Her images are shamed; / her idols are panic-stricken."	Revelation 18:2 "Fallen, fallen is Babylon the great! She has become a home for demons and a lair for every unclean spirit."
Vessel of intoxication	Jeremiah 51:7-8 "Babylon was a gold cup / in the LORD's hand; / it made the whole earth drunk. / The nations drank her wine / and went mad. / But suddenly Babylon fell / and shattered into pieces. / Wail for her!"	Revelation 14:8 "Another angel, a second one, followed and said, 'Fallen, fallen is Babylon the great! She made all the nations drink the wine of her lustful passion.'"

The report of the angel sounds mysterious to us today but would have been clear to the followers of John: "Five kings have fallen, the one is, and the other hasn't yet come. When that king comes, he must remain for only a short time" (Revelation 17:10). These seven kings are followed by an eighth, who is "the beast that was and is not"—perhaps Nero, back from the dead—one who is fortunately "going to destruction" (17:11). The angel then says that the ten horns represent ten additional kings (probably local governors) who have not yet received royal power but will eventually receive power and authority and will give it to the beast (17:12-13).

As frightening as this sounds, the conclusion of the angel's story is hopeful: The kings and the beast "will make war on the Lamb, but the Lamb will emerge victorious, for he is Lord of lords and King of kings" (Revelation 17:14). In the end, Christ the true king will conquer the Roman emperor and his allies, destroying an oppressive military and economic power. The victors will be the Lamb and his followers, those "called, chosen, and faithful" people who have resisted the seduction of Rome (17:14). These words of the angel offer comfort and encouragement to the people of God.

Turmoil in Rome

The wicked prostitute is oppressing the common people of the Roman Empire. The angel observes that she "is seated" (literally sitting) on "peoples, crowds, nations, and languages" (Revelation 17:15). This kind of pressure leads to revolt, which was seen in the history of civil wars between Roman leaders.

The angel says that the ten horns (local governors) and beast will show their hatred for the prostitute by destroying her, stripping her, devouring her flesh, and burning her with fire. They will do this because "God moved them to carry out his purposes" (Revelation 17:17). Clearly, God is active in history; and even evil forces can be instruments of God's purposes. The angel predicts that the fall of Rome is coming soon; and to clarify the identity of the prostitute, he says, "The woman whom you saw is the great city that rules over the kings of the earth" (17:18).

About the Scripture

The Kings (Emperors) of Rome

From Revelation:	From Roman history:
"The seven heads are seven mountains on which the woman is seated. They are also seven kings" (17:9).	Rome was built on seven hills: Palatine, Capitoline, Quirinal, Viminal, Esquiline, Caelian, and Aventine.
	Five kings (emperors) were deified by the Roman Senate, while Domitian claimed to be divine. There were other emperors who reigned between some of these six; but these six are the ones to whom the claim of divinity was attached, a claim that caused problems for Christians, who believed in one God only.
"Five kings have fallen..." (17:10) Fallen king 1	 Julius Caesar (101–44 B.C.)
Fallen king 2	Augustus (31 B.C.–A.D. 14)
Fallen king 3	Claudius (41–54)
Fallen king 4	Vespasian (69–79)
Fallen king 5	Titus (79–81)
Present king 6 "...the one is..." (17:10)	Domitian (81–96)
Coming kings 7 and 8 "...and the other hasn't yet come. When that king comes, he must remain for only a short time" (17:10). "As for the beast that was and is not, it is itself an eighth king that belongs to the seven" (17:11).	Perhaps connected to legends about Nero's return from death (see "The Beast From the Land" in Chapter 4 of this study).

The Fall of Babylon

Another angel comes down from heaven and fills the earth with light. With a voice of great authority, he speaks an announcement of doom: "Fallen, fallen is Babylon the great!" (Revelation 18:2). He describes her spiritual, physical, and moral degradation and concludes with the pronouncement, "The kings of the earth committed sexual immorality with her, and the merchants of the earth became rich from the power of her loose and extravagant ways" (18:3). Because of extensive political and economic corruption, the fall of Rome is sure.

Then another voice from heaven calls for God's people to escape the doomed city: "Come out of her, my people, so that you don't take part in her sins and don't receive any of her plagues. Her sins have piled up as high as heaven, and God remembered her unjust acts" (Revelation 18:4-5). The voice predicts that she will be punished by deadly disease, grief, and hunger and that she will be "consumed by fire because the Lord God who judges her is powerful" (18:8). While Rome might consider herself a powerful city, she is no match for almighty God.

Mourning by Kings, Merchants, and Seafarers

Of course, not everyone will celebrate the fall of Rome. Those who have been enriched by the wicked city will mourn her passing. First to weep will be the kings of the earth, who shared her loose and extravagant ways. They "will weep and mourn over her when they see the smoke from her burning. They will stand a long way off because they are afraid of the pain she suffers, and they will say, 'Oh, the horror! Babylon, you great city, you powerful city! In a single hour your judgment has come.'" (18:9-10). This apparently invincible city will be destroyed in a single hour by a firestorm of divine wrath.

Second to mourn are the merchants of the earth, "for no one buys their cargoes anymore" (Revelation 18:11). They will lose their wealthy trading partner, the city that buys their "cargoes of gold, silver, jewels, and pearls; fine linen, purple, silk, and scarlet; all those things made of scented wood, ivory, fine wood, bronze, iron, and marble; cinnamon, incense, fragrant ointment, and frankincense; wine, oil, fine flour, and wheat; cattle, sheep, horses, and carriages, and slaves, even human lives" (18:12-13).

The voice from heaven offers this long and highly detailed list to show how the glamour and riches of the whole world are gathered in Rome, a place that has a market for everything, including slaves and human lives. The city is the very peak of human accomplishment, the New York City or Tokyo of its day. And yet it will fall suddenly, catching people by surprise because it has rotted from within. "All your glitter and glamour are lost to you," says the voice from heaven, "never ever to be found again" (Revelation 18:14).

Like the kings, the merchants who got rich by the city will weep, mourn, and say, "Oh, the horror! The great city that wore fine linen, purple, and scarlet, who glittered with gold, jewels, and pearls—in just one hour such great wealth was destroyed" (Revelation 18:16-17). The voice from heaven is warning us about the transience of worldly wealth and how quickly it can be taken from us. Every book in the New Testament talks about wealth and its dangers, including Revelation. When lured by material goods, it is critically important that we not forget God.

Third to grieve are the sea captains, seafarers, sailors, and all who make their living on the sea. They will cry out because there was a port near Rome that made them rich. "What city was ever like the great city?" they ask. "The great city, where all who have ships at sea became so rich by her prosperity—in just one hour she was destroyed. Rejoice over her, heaven—you saints, apostles, and prophets—because God has condemned her as she condemned you" (Revelation 18:18-20). The citizens of heaven are invited to rejoice over the condemnation of the city that condemned the saints, the apostles, and the prophets.

The End of an Era

In a powerful symbolic act, an angel picks up a stone that is like a huge millstone and throws it into the sea, saying, "With such violent force the great city of Babylon will be thrown down, and it won't be found anymore" (Revelation 18:21). He predicts that the sound of musicians will never again be heard in the city, nor will craftsmen be found working.

The sound of the hand mill will never again be heard, nor the sound of a bridegroom and a bride. There will not even be the light of a lamp in the city (18:22-23). Every sign of life will be eliminated, from the musical and the industrial to the deeply personal. All will be silent, and all will be dark.

And why is this? Because "your merchants ran the world," says the angel, "because all the nations were deceived by the spell you cast, and because the blood of prophets, of saints, and of all who have been slaughtered on the earth was found among you," the great city of Rome (Revelation 18:23-24).

God passed judgment on Rome because its merchants ran the world by exploiting people and resources throughout a global economy. Nations were deceived by its seductive promise of wealth and power and entered into alliances that were no healthier than sleeping with a prostitute. Roman justice was enforced by vast military power, and people who took a principled stand against the imperial cult—the prophets and saints of the church—often paid with their lives. John challenges Christians of every age to serve God instead of earthly powers and to resist the temptation of wealth that is associated with loose and extravagant ways.

Live the Story

An advertisement for a new dress, stunning in scarlet and purple. A jewelry store window, glittering with gold, jewels, and pearls. A showcase containing the latest electronic gadget, affordable because it was assembled by workers in the developing world. All these material goods are tempting, but we wonder where they come from and whether people and resources were exploited in their production. International alliances can be complicated and morally questionable in our vast global economy.

In the Book of Revelation, John discovers that God will bring judgment on powers that gain their wealth through political and economic oppression. He challenges Christians to resist the lure of materialism and to see that the glitter of this world is tempting and attractive, but it leads to destruction. Only by focusing on God do we find the way that leads to life.

We express our beliefs every time we open our wallets. When you go to the store and see an item that you want (but do not really need), will you pull out your credit card and buy it, or will you resist the temptation? When you pay your bills for the month, will you include support for church and charity in your regular expenditures? God is concerned about your spending patterns and wants to be the Lord of both your money and your life.

1. From *Five Practices: Extravagant Generosity*, by Robert Schnase (Abingdon Press, 2008); page 29.

2. From "Dave's Best Guests from 2010," January 6, 2011, Dave Ramsey Website, http://www.daveramsey.com/article/daves-best-guests-from-2010/lifeandmoney_other/text1/. (4-26-11)

God Is in Control

Revelation 19–20

Claim Your Story

Michael Vick was flying high as a superstar NFL quarterback, but he crashed to earth when he was sent to prison for playing a role in a savage dog-fighting ring. Realizing that football could not save him, he made a public apology: "I'm upset with myself and, you know, through this situation I found Jesus and asked him for forgiveness and turned my life over to God."[1]

Many people laughed at his apology, thinking that it was insincere and designed to gain public sympathy. But when Vick emerged from prison, he seemed to be a truly changed man. He admits that before he was incarcerated, "it was all about me." But his faith in God enabled him to get through prison. "Now I'm more at peace," he says. "God has taken it over. I don't have to worry about being dynamic. God is in control of that."[2]

With God in control, Vick has restarted a truly dynamic football career. His story can teach us several important lessons when we are in the midst of trouble. First, evildoers will get their comeuppance—Vick did twenty-one months in prison. But second, and more importantly, holding fast to God brings real comfort. Your story, like Michael Vick's, will take a turn for the better if you put your complete faith in God.

Enter the Bible Story

John hears what sounds like a huge crowd in heaven, celebrating the power of God and the punishment of "the great prostitute," the city of Rome (Revelation 19:2). The first six verses of Chapter 19 are a poetic commentary on Chapters 17 and 18, with the voices of heaven singing,

> Hallelujah! [literally, "Praise God!"] The salvation and glory
>   and power of our God!
> His judgments are true and just,
>   because he judged the great prostitute,
>   who ruined the earth by her whoring,
> and he exacted the penalty for the blood of his servants from
>   her hand. (19:1-2)

The heavenly crowd praises God for the smoke that goes up from the burning of Rome, and the twenty-four elders and four living creatures (see Revelation 4:2-7) add their "Amen. Hallelujah!" (19:3-4).

Then a voice from the throne says, "Praise our God, all you his servants, / and you who fear him, both small and great" (Revelation 19:5, an echo of Psalm 115:13). And the crowd of God's servants responds with praise, "Hallelujah! The Lord our God, the Almighty, / exercised his royal power!" (19:6). Looking back on the judgment and punishment of Rome, the residents of heaven see that God is in control.

The Lamb and His Bride

The heavenly crowd suddenly shifts its attention from a prostitute to a bride. They say,

> Let us rejoice and celebrate, and give him the glory,
>   for the wedding day of the Lamb has come,
>   and his bride has made herself ready.
> She was given fine, pure white linen to wear,
>   for the fine linen is the saints' acts of justice.
>   (Revelation 19:7-8)

The Lamb is Jesus; and his bride is the church (Ephesians 5:23-32), made pure and beautiful by the acts of justice performed by the saints. The phrase "acts of justice" appears also in Revelation 15:4, referring to the work of God. Here, on this day of the wedding between the bride and the Lamb, the work of the saints reflects the work of God, making it possible for the church to enter into a deep and intimate relationship with Jesus Christ.

About the Christian Faith

The Bride of Christ

Identity: The Church

The apostle Paul first uses this image in his letter to the Ephesians, when he advises husbands and wives to have a relationship modeled on the loving bond between Christ and the church: "As for husbands, love your wives just like Christ loved the church and gave himself for her" (Ephesians 5:25).

Behavior: Acts of Justice

John picks up on this image in Revelation when he reports that a voice from the heavenly throne says, "Let us rejoice and celebrate, and give him the glory, / for the wedding day of the Lamb has come, / and his bride has made herself ready. / She was given fine, pure white linen to wear, / for the fine linen is the saints' acts of justice" (Revelation 19:7-8). Here the beauty and purity of the bride (church) comes from acts of justice done in loving service to the groom (Lamb/Christ).

In the Future: New Creation

Finally, one of the seven angels of Revelation says to John, "I will show you the bride, the Lamb's wife"; and he takes him to a high mountain to see "the holy city, Jerusalem, coming down out of heaven from God" (Revelation 21:9-10). Here the bride of Christ is part of the new creation, the place where God will dwell eternally.

In the Present: Christian Marriage

In all of these images, the relationship between Christ and his bride is one of love, commitment, intimacy, and sacrificial service, which is why Christian weddings often draw a parallel between the bond of marriage and "the mystery of the union between Christ and his Church" (Book of Common Prayer [Episcopal], 1979).

An angel then commands John to take dictation. "Write this: Favored are those who have been invited to the wedding banquet of the Lamb" (Revelation 19:9). John falls at his feet to worship him; but the angel objects, saying, "Don't do that! I'm a servant just like you and your brothers and sisters who hold firmly to the witness of Jesus. Worship God! The witness of Jesus is the spirit of prophecy!" (19:10).

Angels and faithful humans are equal servants of Christ; and both groups are challenged to worship God, embrace the testimony of Jesus, and share prophetic messages such as are found in Revelation. John knows that faithfulness can be costly, since he is on the island of Patmos because of his "witness about Jesus" (Revelation 1:9). In every time and place, faithfulness to Christ can cause us to become isolated from the larger culture.

Christ Defeats the Beast and His Armies

Heaven opens, and John sees Jesus on a white horse (Revelation 19:11). Jesus is once again the Divine Warrior of Revelation 1:13-16, judging fairly, making wars justly, and bearing the names "Faithful and True" (19:11). His eyes are like "a fiery flame," his head bears many royal crowns, and he has a mysterious name written on him "that no one knows but he himself" (19:12-13)—perhaps the personal name of God revealed in Exodus 3:13-14 or the "name above all names" of Philippians 2:9. Jesus wears a robe dyed with the blood of his death on the cross, and his name is called "the Word of God" (Revelation 19:13, compare John 1:1-14).

The angelic armies of heaven, wearing linen as white and pure as the garment of the bride of Christ, follow him on white horses (Revelation 19:14). Into battle they go, behind the Divine Warrior who once again has "a sharp sword that he will use to strike down the nations" (19:15). Jesus is the one who will rule with an iron rod and "trample the winepress of the Almighty God's passionate anger" (19:15), repeating the harvest of judgment of Revelation 14:17-20 and offering an image that continues to inspire us in "The Battle Hymn of the Republic." To show his power over all the rulers of the earth, Jesus has a name written on his robe and on his thigh: "King of kings and Lord of lords" (19:16). Christ is mightier than Caesar, far greater than any of the leaders of the earth—past or present.

These names and qualities describe different aspects of the character of Christ in God's divine drama. Jesus is clearly higher than the angels, with a special link to God. His mysterious name, in particular, sends the message that he cannot be controlled. Like God, he simply is who he is and will be who he will be (Exodus 3:14). This is an important quality as the battle with evil intensifies.

Divine Names

Name	God	Christ
Faithful and True	Deuteronomy 7:9 "Know now then that the LORD your God is the only true God! He is the faithful God, who keeps the covenant and proves loyal to everyone who loves him and keeps his commands—even to the thousandth generation!"	Revelation 19:11 "Then I saw heaven opened, and there was a white horse. Its rider was called Faithful and True, and he judges and makes war justly."
Mysterious name	Exodus 3:13-14 "But Moses said to God, 'If I now come to the Israelites and say to them, "The God of your ancestors has sent me to you," they are going to ask me, "What's this God's name?" What am I supposed to say to them?' God said to Moses, 'I Am Who I Am. So say to the Israelites, "I Am has sent me to you."'"	Revelation 19:12 "His eyes were like a fiery flame, and on his head were many royal crowns. He has a name written on him that no one knows but himself."
Lord and King	Esther, Addition c, verse 8 (from the Greek version, found in the Apocrypha) "Now, Lord God, King, God of Abraham, spare your people, because the enemy seeks our ruin."	Revelation 19:16 "He has a name written on his robe and on his thigh: King of kings and Lord of lords."

John sees an angel standing in the sun, one who calls to all the birds of prey flying overhead, "Come and gather for God's great supper" (Revelation 19:17). His invitation is gruesome: "Come and eat the flesh of kings, the flesh of generals, the flesh of the powerful, and the flesh of horses and their riders. Come and eat the flesh of all, both free and slave, both small and great" (19:18). Sure enough, a bloody buffet is provided by the battle that follows.

The beast (the Roman Empire), the kings of the earth, and their armies gather to make war against Christ and his army (Revelation 19:19). But the beast is seized, along with "the false prophet" who is the beast from the land in Revelation 13:11-15—probably the high priest of the imperial cult "who had done signs in the beast's presence" (19:20). The beast and false prophet are thrown alive into the fiery lake that burns with sulfur; and the rest are "killed by the sword that comes from the mouth of the rider on the horse," leaving their bodies to be eaten by the birds (19:20-21).

Satan Is Confined

Another angel comes down from heaven, "holding in his hand the key to the abyss and a huge chain" (Revelation 20:1). He seizes "the dragon, the old snake, who is the devil and Satan," and binds him for a thousand years (20:2). Satan is thrown into the abyss, which is then locked and sealed over so that Satan cannot continue to deceive the nations until the thousand years are over (20:3a). "After this," says John, "he must be released for a little while" (20:3b).

This thousand-year period of Satan's confinement is a break from supernatural warfare and a refreshing breather for the people of the world. Christ rules completely, with no threats from evil empires. The term "Millennialism" comes from this thousand-year period and refers to a golden age of Christ's rule before the Final Judgment. Of course, Christians today are not in agreement about when and how Christ will appear, leading to divisions between Premillennialists (those who believe that Jesus will physically be on earth for his millennial reign), Amillennialists (those who believe that Christ's reign during the millennium is spiritual, not physical), and Postmillennialists (those who believe that the second coming of Jesus will occur after the millennium).

Millennial debates aside, why is Satan given another chance by God? Why not destroy him immediately? This time of captivity reminds us that Satan is one of God's creatures—a fallen angel, not a divine being who is equal to God. Satan is confined to show that God is in control. Also, when Satan is released, he is given a second chance by a loving, merciful, and compassionate God. But Satan fails the test.

The story of Job is a useful comparison. Satan (the "Adversary") predicts that Job will not be righteous when he is tested (Job 1:11), but Job is. In Revelation, God gives Satan a chance to be righteous when he is tested; and Satan is not.

The Saints Come to Life and Reign With Christ

Then John sees people take seats on thrones. They are the saints "who had been beheaded for their witness to Jesus and God's word" (Revelation 20:4; recall the martyrs of Revelation 6:9-10), as well as those who had resisted worshiping the beast and receiving its mark. The saints come to life and reign with Christ for a thousand years (20:4). "This is the first resurrection," says John. "Favored and holy are those who have a share in the first resurrection. The second death has no power over them, but they will be priests of God and of Christ, and will reign with him for a thousand years" (20:5-6). The rest of the dead don't come to life until the thousand years are over, and then they face the possibility of a "second death" after the Final Judgment.

Satan Is Defeated

When the thousand years are over, Satan is released from his prison. He immediately fails the test of righteousness by going out to deceive the nations that are at the four corners of the earth (Gog and Magog). Satan gathers them for battle; and they surround the saints' camp in Jerusalem, "the city that God loves" (Revelation 20:7-9a).

About the Scripture

Resurrection

Old Testament / Early New Testament	The return of the dead to life through resurrection does not play a large role in the Old Testament.
	There was a lively debate about it in New Testament times—according to Matthew, "That same day Sadducees, who deny that there is a resurrection, came to Jesus" (22:23).
Ministry of Jesus	Jesus is in the pro-resurrection camp and predicts, "Those who did good things will come out into the resurrection of life, and those who did wicked things into the resurrection of judgment" (John 5:29).
	When Jesus is talking with Martha after the death of her brother Lazarus, Martha says, "I know that he will rise in the resurrection on the last day." Jesus shifts her expectations by saying, "I am the resurrection and the life. Whoever believes in me will live, even though they die" (John 11:24-25).
Early Church	The connection between Jesus and resurrection is strengthened by his own return to life on what we now call Easter and then reinforced by the teaching of the apostles:
	"If we were united together in a death like his, we will also be united together in a resurrection like his" (Romans 6:5).
	"You have been born anew into a living hope through the resurrection of Jesus Christ from the dead" (1 Peter 1:3).
Revelation	Those who are faithful to Christ are promised resurrection in Revelation, including those "who had been beheaded for their witness to Jesus" (20:4). They are given "a share in the first resurrection" and "will be priests of God and of Christ" (20:6).
	The second resurrection occurs later, prior to the Final Judgment (20:11-15), and includes "the rest of the dead" (20:5).

But God is in complete control, and he deals directly and decisively with Satan. Fire comes down from heaven and consumes the armies; and the deceiving devil is "thrown into the lake of fire and sulfur," where the beast and the false prophet reside. Painful suffering is inflicted on them "day and night, forever and ever" (Revelation 20:9b-10). The old snake is finally crushed. The ultimate evildoer gets his comeuppance.

The Final Judgment

Then John sees "a great white throne and the one who is seated on it" (Revelation 20:11). Before his face both earth and heaven flee away, and no place is found for them—the second resurrection is occurring. John sees the dead standing before the throne; and scrolls are opened, including "the Scroll of Life." The dead are judged on the basis of what is written in the scrolls about their deeds (20:11-12).

The sea gives up its dead, as do "Death and the Grave" (Revelation 1:18). People are judged by what they have done (20:13), much as Jesus had predicted when he said, "the Human One is about to come with the majesty of his Father with his angels. And then he will repay each one for what that person has done" (Matthew 16:27).

Then Death and the Grave are thrown into the fiery lake, along with anyone whose name isn't found written in the scroll of life. "This, the fiery lake, is the second death," says John, the final condemnation of sinners (Resurrection 20:14-15). Throughout this process, God and Christ are in complete control.

Live the Story

"Forgive us our trespasses, as we forgive those who trespass against us." This line from the Lord's Prayer reminds us that we all have been perpetrators of evil and that we all have been victims as well. Either way, we know that evil does great damage, throwing our lives into turmoil and distancing us from God, from our neighbors, and from our own best selves. As Michael Vick said about his life before his incarceration, "It was all about me."

Revelation promises us that evildoers will get their comeuppance, but this is small comfort when profound injury has been done to us by another person or when we ourselves are bearing a heavy burden of guilt. In the end, holding fast to God brings real comfort because God is in control of all of life—including the possibility of forgiveness, healing, restoration, and reconciliation.

In the troubles you face at home or at work, hold firmly to Jesus. He is the one who can offer you forgiveness and peace. Turn your life over to God, who has the power to preserve and protect you. Follow the lead of the saints of the church, who can teach you acts of justice. And put your complete trust in God and Christ, the ones who offer all their faithful servants the gift of everlasting life.

1. From http://sports.espn.go.com/nfl/news/story?id=2993103. (4-20-11)
2. From http://www.christianindex.org/6259.article. (4-20-11)

All Things New

Revelation 21–22

Claim Your Story

The casket is surrounded by flowers. The grieving family is seated in the front row; and the preacher says, "God loves us so much that he does not want our existence to end with the death of our bodies. No, he wants our lives to continue in his everlasting kingdom, that place where there is neither illness nor crying, pain nor dying. 'Look! I'm making all things new' (Revelation 21:5), says the Lord of all creation. God is working to bring us all to a better place, a place where we can be closer to him and to one another, free from anything that can hurt or divide us."

Words like these are often heard at Christian funerals because the last two chapters of Revelation are a source of tremendous comfort and hope in times of grief. We believe in the Resurrection, yes; the raising of Jesus gives us the assurance that death is not the end. But we also believe in a divine restoration in which everything is made new and trouble free.

Resurrection would be ultimately unsatisfying if it simply returned us to a life of illness, suffering, and pain. The good news is that God is creating a new heaven and a new earth, free from the agonies of this life. Know that as a follower of Jesus you have a future that looks radically different from the present—nothing less than the restoration of Eden!

Enter the Bible Story

The promise of Revelation 21–22 is a new relationship with God, one that is both intimate and eternal. This bond is a restoration of the original creation in Genesis and contains the best of numerous biblical images and understandings of the divine-human covenant, particularly from the Old Testament.

New Heaven, New Earth

As Chapter 21 begins, John sees "a new heaven and a new earth, for the former heaven and the former earth had passed away, and the sea was no more" (Revelation 21:1). God first revealed this vision through the prophet Isaiah, saying,

> Look! I'm creating
> a new heaven and a new earth:
> past events won't be remembered;
> they won't come to mind. (Isaiah 65:17)

> As the new heavens
> and the new earth that I'm making
> will endure before me, says the LORD,
> so your descendants
> and your name will endure. (Isaiah 66:22)

This new creation is one in which the past is forgotten and the future endures forever. Even the sea, described in Chapter 4 of this study as the home of the beast and a symbol of watery chaos, is "no more" (Revelation 21:1). This renewed and transformed creation fulfills the expectation of the apostle Paul that "the creation itself will be set free from slavery to decay and brought into the glorious freedom of God's children" (Romans 8:21).

John sees "the holy city, New Jerusalem, coming down out of heaven from God, made ready as a bride beautifully dressed for her husband" (Revelation 21:2). New Jerusalem is the new covenant that God has made with the followers of Christ. Paul says that "the Jerusalem that is above is free, and she is our mother" (Galatians 4:26). This holy city can also be seen as the church, the bride of Christ (see Chapter 7 of this study). But most importantly, New Jerusalem is the beautiful place where God and humans will live together eternally.

The voice of God speaks from the throne: "Look! God's dwelling is here with humankind. He will dwell with them, and they will be his peoples. God himself will be with them as their God" (Revelation 21:3). These words are the language of covenant, updating the promise-based relationship first established when God said to Abraham, "I will be your God and your descendants' God after you" (Genesis 17:7) and reaffirmed through the prophet Ezekiel: "My dwelling will be with them, and I will be their God, and they will be my people" (Ezekiel 37:27).

After long years of struggle—with humans frequently breaking their covenant with God—the promise is made that God "will wipe away every tear from their eyes. Death will be no more. There will be no mourning, crying, or pain anymore, for the former things have passed away" (Revelation 21:4). The covenant will be renewed, for all eternity.

Then God says, "Look! I'm making all things new"; and he instructs John to write down his true and trustworthy words (Revelation 21:5). God proclaims, "All is done. I am the Alpha and the Omega" (21:6), using the same words of self-description that he used in Revelation 1:8. Alpha and Omega are the first and last letters of the Greek alphabet, the language used in Revelation. So God is saying, in effect, "I am the A and the Z, the beginning and the end."

Echoing Isaiah and Jesus, God then says, "To the thirsty I will freely give water from the life-giving spring" (Revelation 21:6). The prophet had said, "All of you who are thirsty, / come to the water!" (Isaiah 55:1); and Jesus had said, "The water that I give will become in those who drink it a spring of water that bubbles up into eternal life" (John 4:14). This offer of gracious hospitality extends to those "who emerge victorious," faithful men and women who will be God's "sons and daughters" (Revelation 21:7); and the result is that they are given a new relationship with God.

But the free gift of life-giving water is not extended to a list of sinners, ranging from the cowardly to liars. God says that they will be tossed into "the lake that burns with fire and sulfur"—"the second death" (Revelation 21:8; compare 20:14-15).

New Jerusalem

Next, one of the seven angels (see Chapter 5 of this study) invites John to see "the bride, the Lamb's wife" (Revelation 21:9). He takes John "in a Spirit-inspired trance [as in 1:10] to a great, high mountain" and shows him "the holy city, Jerusalem, coming down out of heaven from God" (21:10). This New Jerusalem contains "God's glory" (21:11) and is clearly the place of God's dwelling. It has "a great high wall with twelve gates," twelve angels, the names of the twelve tribes of Israel, and twelve foundations containing the "names of the Lamb's twelve apostles" (21:12-14). This number is significant because of the twelve tribes of Israel and the twelve apostles of Christ and is emphasized repeatedly in the structure of the city itself.

The angel who speaks to John has "a golden measuring rod with which to measure the city, its gates, and its wall" (Revelation 21:15); and it quickly becomes clear that the New Jerusalem has roots in both the glory of the Temple of Solomon and the Jerusalem of Old Testament times. The city is "laid out as a square" (21:16) and is "pure gold, like pure glass" (21:18).

The foundations of the city wall are "decorated with every kind of jewel"—from jasper to amethyst (Revelation 21:19-20)—precious stones that did not actually decorate the foundations of old Jerusalem but stand as a fulfillment of the prophecy of Isaiah,

> I am setting your gemstones in silvery metal
> and your foundations with sapphires.
> I will make your towers of rubies,
> and your gates of beryl,
> and all your walls of precious jewels. (Isaiah 54:11-12)

Old Jerusalem and New Jerusalem

The Glory of God	1 Kings 8:1, 10-11 "Then Solomon assembled Israel's elders, all the tribal leaders, and the chiefs of Israel's clans at Jerusalem to bring up the chest containing the LORD's covenant from David's City Zion.... The cloud filled the LORD's temple, and the priests were unable to carry out their duties due to the cloud because the LORD's glory filled the LORD's temple."	Revelation 21:9-11 "Then one of the seven angels who had the seven bowls full of the seven last plagues spoke with me. 'Come,' he said, 'I will show you the bride, the Lamb's wife.' He took me in a Spirit-inspired trance to a great, high mountain, and he showed me the holy city, Jerusalem, coming down out of heaven from God. The city had God's glory."
Covered in Gold	1 Kings 6:21-22 "Solomon covered the temple's interior with pure gold. He placed gold chains in front of the inner sanctuary and covered it with gold. He overlaid the whole temple inside with gold until the temple was completely covered. He covered the whole altar that was in the inner sanctuary with gold."	Revelation 21:15, 18, 21 "The angel who spoke to me had a golden measuring rod with which to measure the city, its gates, and its wall.... The wall was built of jasper, and the city was pure gold, like pure glass.... And the city's main street was pure gold, as transparent as glass."
Precious Treasures	2 Chronicles 9:22-24, 27 "King Solomon far exceeded all the earth's kings in wealth and wisdom, and kings of every nation wanted an audience with Solomon in order to hear his God-given wisdom. Year after year they came with tribute: objects of silver and gold, clothing, weapons, spices, horses, and mules.... In Jerusalem, the king made silver as common as stones and cedar as common as sycamore trees that grow in the foothills."	Revelation 21:19-20 "The city wall's foundations were decorated with every kind of jewel. The first foundation was jasper, the second was sapphire, the third was chalcedony, and the fourth was emerald. The fifth was sardonyx, the sixth was carnelian, the seventh was chrysolite, and the eighth was beryl. The ninth was topaz, the tenth was chrysoprase, the eleventh was jacinth, and the twelfth was amethyst."
Wide and Large	Nehemiah 7:4 "Now although the city was wide and large, only a few people were living within it, and no houses had been rebuilt."	Revelation 21:16 "Now the city was laid out as a square. Its length was the same as its width. He measured the city with a rod, and it was fifteen hundred miles."

The twelve gates of New Jerusalem are "twelve pearls"; and the city's main street is "pure gold, as transparent as glass" (Revelation 21:21).

These precious jewels, pearls, and gold are symbols of the treasures in heaven that Jesus encourages us to collect for ourselves in the Sermon on the Mount (Matthew 6:20). Simply put, they are the precious qualities of our relationship with God. In eternal significance, such heavenly treasures exceed all of the wealth of the Roman Empire (compare the treasures of Rome listed in Revelation 18:12-13).

No Temple in New Jerusalem

John sees no "temple in the city, because its temple is the Lord God Almighty and the Lamb" (Revelation 21:22). Unlike old Jerusalem, there is no need for a temple because in New Jerusalem people are given direct access to God and the Lamb. There is not even a need for the sun and the moon because "God's glory is its light, and its lamp is the Lamb" (21:23). The glory of God and the Lamb (Jesus, the "light of the world" [John 8:12]) provide sufficient light to guide the nations of the earth in perpetual illumination (21:24-25). New Jerusalem is the servant of the Lord described by the prophet Isaiah, "a covenant to the people . . . a light to the nations" (Isaiah 42:6). In this eternal city, faithful people will live forever in the presence of God; and nothing unclean will ever enter it, "nor anyone who does what is vile and deceitful, but only those who are registered in the Lamb's scroll of life" (Revelation 21:27).

New Jerusalem contains the fulfillment of many Old Testament dreams. In the Creation story, a "river flows from Eden to water the garden" (Genesis 2:10). In Revelation, the angel shows John "the river of life-giving water [or "the water of life"], shining like crystal, flowing from the throne of God and the Lamb through the middle of the city's main street" (Revelation 22:1-2). In Eden, "the LORD God grew every beautiful tree with edible fruit, and also he grew the tree of life in the middle of the garden" (Genesis 2:9). Further on in the Old Testament, the prophet Ezekiel has a vision in which a river flows through the temple, with fruit-bearing trees on the banks of the river—their "fruit will be for eating, their leaves for healing" (Ezekiel 47:12). In New Jerusalem, on "each side of the river is the tree of life.... The tree's leaves are for the healing of the nations" (Revelation 22:2). This is the place where creation is renewed, brokenness is healed, and curses are removed (22:3).

Best of all, the "throne of God and the Lamb will be in it, and his servants will worship him. They will see his face" (Revelation 22:3-4). Faithful people will finally encounter God and Christ directly, as the apostle Paul dreamed when he wrote, "Now we see a reflection in a mirror; then we will see face-to-face" (1 Corinthians 13:12). The light of God will shine directly on those who worship him, and together the Lord and his servants will "reign forever and ever" (Revelation 22:5).

Jesus Is Coming Soon

The Book of Revelation begins with Jesus sending an angel to John with a message (1:1). An angel (perhaps the same one) now reminds John that the God of the spirits of the prophets "sent his angel to show his servants what must soon take place" (22:6). Then Jesus himself says, "Look! I'm coming soon. Favored is the one who keeps the words of the prophecy contained in this scroll" (22:7). He reinforces the importance of reading and observing the prophecies contained in the Book of Revelation (compare 1:3).

Now John speaks for himself, saying, "I, John, am the one who heard and saw these things" (Revelation 22:8). He is an eyewitness to these visions from heaven, with the words of Revelation offered as personal testimony. John's reaction to this supernatural experience is to fall down and worship at the feet of the angel; but the angel says, "Don't do that! I'm a servant just like you.... Worship God!" (22:8-9). As in 19:10, the angel admits that he is simply a fellow servant of the Lord and tells John to direct his worship to God. Then he commands, "Don't seal up the words of the prophecy contained in this scroll, because the time is near" (22:10). The end is so close that people will have no time to change their behavior (22:11).

The voice of Jesus is heard again, "Look! I'm coming soon," to act as a judge and "repay all people as their actions deserve" (Revelation 22:12). Jesus applies God's title to himself—"I am the Alpha and the Omega"—

and offers a blessing (beatitude) to the martyrs who have washed their robes in blood (see 7:14) and now "may have the right of access to the tree of life and may enter the city [New Jerusalem] by the gates" (22:13-14). By using God's title, Jesus reveals that he is in control of history and is Lord of the world. He and God are united in their acceptance of those who have suffered for the faith and in their rejection of those who persist in sin, including "drug users" and "all who love and practice deception" (22:15).

About the Scripture

Beatitudes

In Revelation 22:14, Jesus says, "Favored are [NRSV, Blessed are] those who wash their robes so that they may have the right of access to the tree of life and may enter the city by the gates." This is a beatitude, similar to the first lines of the Sermon on the Mount: "Happy are [NRSV, Blessed are] people who are downcast, because the kingdom of heaven is theirs..." (Matthew 5:3 and following). Such expressions are promises that spiritual rewards will come to those who suffer external tribulations or internal difficulties. Beatitudes also appear in Revelation 1:3, 14:13, 16:15, 19:9, 20:6, and 22:7.

Testify!

Jesus concludes by saying that he has sent his angel "to bear witness to all of you about these things for the churches" (Revelation 22:16). To bear witness is to testify, to speak the truth, which is what the angel has done and what John of Patmos is doing. It is what we are challenged to do as well.

"I'm the root and descendant of David," says Jesus, "the bright morning star" (Revelation 22:16). Jesus is the one who fulfills Isaiah 11:1 ("shoot...from the stump of Jesse") and Matthew 1:1 ("Jesus Christ, son of David").

The Spirit and the bride (church) say to Jesus, "Come!" (Revelation 22:17a). Then John invites the one who hears these words to say to Jesus, "Come!" (22:17b). And he invites the one who is thirsty to "receive life-giving water" (22:17c). John extends the invitation that had been offered by Jesus during his ministry: "All who are thirsty should come to me!" (John 7:37).

"Now I bear witness [testify] to everyone who hears the words of the prophecy contained in this scroll," says John. "If anyone adds to them, God will add to that person the plagues that are written in this scroll. If anyone takes away from the words of this scroll of prophecy, God will take away that person's share in the tree of life and the holy city" (Revelation 22:18-19). John warns against doing anything that will corrupt the testimony that he has given in this book.

Jesus, the one who "bears witness" to these things, says, "Yes, I'm coming soon." And John answers, in a prayer of the early church, "Amen. Come, Lord Jesus!" (Revelation 22:20). The he closes with the words, "The grace of the Lord Jesus be with all" (22:21).

Live the Story

Funeral services often contain Revelation's vision of a new heaven and a new earth, and these verses bring comfort when we have lost a friend or a loved one. The promise that "death will be no more" gives hope for the future; and the assurance that God "will wipe away every tear" offers the assurance of eternal, compassionate care (Revelation 21:4).

But what difference does this make when you return home from the funeral? How does the restoration of Eden impact the living of your days? For starters, Revelation shows that God wants a new relationship with you, one that is intimate and eternal. God desires open and honest communication with you, through prayer and worship. The Lord does not want you to suffer forever but is actively working to heal and save you.

Revelation also leaves you with a challenge: to bear witness, to testify, to speak the truth. The angel of the book does this, as does John of Patmos and Jesus himself. In a long line of faithful witnesses, you are in the next group being called on to speak the truth about Jesus, the one who is Lord of all.

The message of Revelation is that Jesus comes to you as Lord. He is the one who rules over today's world and the coming New Jerusalem, over this life and everlasting life. Christian faith requires that we serve the Lord who makes all things new, whether we are living in the Roman Empire or in the United States.

In whatever you say and do, testify to this truth.

Leader Guide

People often view the Bible as a maze of obscure people, places, and events from centuries ago and struggle to relate it to their daily lives. IMMERSION invites us to experience the Bible as a record of God's loving revelation to humankind. These studies recognize our emotional, spiritual, and intellectual needs and welcome us into the Bible story and into deeper faith.

As leader of an IMMERSION group, you will help participants to encounter the Word of God and the God of the Word that will lead to new creation in Christ. You do not have to be an expert to lead; in fact, you will participate with your group in listening to and applying God's life-transforming Word to your lives. You and your group will explore the building blocks of the Christian faith through key stories, people, ideas, and teachings in every book of the Bible. You will also explore the bridges and points of connection between the Old and New Testaments.

Choosing and Using the Bible

The central goal of IMMERSION is engaging the members of your group with the Bible in a way that informs their minds, forms their hearts, and transforms the way they live out their Christian faith. Participants will need this study book and a Bible. IMMERSION is an excellent accompaniment to the Common English Bible (CEB). It shares with the CEB four common aims: clarity of language, faith in the Bible's power to transform lives, the emotional expectation that people will find the love of God, and the rational expectation that people will find the knowledge of God.

Other recommended study Bibles include *The New Interpreter's Study Bible* (NRSV), *The New Oxford Annotated Study Bible* (NRSV), *The HarperCollins Study Bible* (NRSV), the *NIV and TNIV Study Bibles*, and the *Archaeological Study Bible* (NIV). Encourage participants to use more than one translation. *The Message: The Bible in Contemporary Language* is a modern paraphrase of the Bible, based on the original languages. Eugene H. Peterson has created a masterful presentation of the Scripture text, which is best used alongside rather than in place of the CEB or another primary English translation.

One of the most reliable interpreters of the Bible's meaning is the Bible itself. Invite participants first of all to allow Scripture to have its say. Pay attention to context. Ask questions of the text. Read every passage with curiosity, always seeking to answer the basic Who? What? Where? When? and Why? questions.

Bible study groups should also have handy essential reference resources in case someone wants more information or needs clarification on specific words, terms, concepts, places, or people mentioned in the Bible. A Bible dictionary, Bible atlas, concordance, and one-volume Bible commentary together make for a good, basic reference library.

The Leader's Role

An effective leader prepares ahead. This leader guide provides easy to follow, step-by-step suggestions for leading a group. The key task of the leader is to guide discussion and activities that will engage heart and head and will invite faith development. Discussion questions are included, and you may want to add questions posed by you or your group. Here are suggestions for helping your group engage Scripture:

State questions clearly and simply.

Ask questions that move Bible truths from "outside" (dealing with concepts, ideas, or information about a passage) to "inside" (relating to the experiences, hopes, and dreams of the participants).

Work for variety in your questions, including compare and contrast, information recall, motivation, connections, speculation, and evaluation.

Avoid questions that call for yes-or-no responses or answers that are obvious.

Don't be afraid of silence during a discussion. It often yields especially thoughtful comments.

Test questions before using them by attempting to answer them yourself.

When leading a discussion, pay attention to the mood of your group by "listening" with your eyes as well as your ears.

Guidelines for the Group

IMMERSION is designed to promote full engagement with the Bible for the purpose of growing faith and building up Christian community. While much can be gained from individual reading, a group Bible study offers an ideal setting in which to achieve these aims. Encourage participants to bring their Bibles and read from Scripture during the session. Invite participants to consider the following guidelines as they participate in the group:

Respect differences of interpretation and understanding.

Support one another with Christian kindness, compassion, and courtesy.

Listen to others with the goal of understanding rather than agreeing or disagreeing.

Celebrate the opportunity to grow in faith through Bible study.

Approach the Bible as a dialogue partner, open to the possibility of being challenged or changed by God's Word.

Recognize that each person brings unique and valuable life experiences to the group and is an important part of the community.

Reflect theologically—that is, be attentive to three basic questions: What does this say about God? What does this say about me/us? What does this say about the relationship between God and me/us?

Commit to a *lived faith response* in light of insights you gain from the Bible. In other words, what changes in attitudes (how you believe) or actions (how you behave) are called for by God's Word?

Group Sessions

The group sessions, like the chapters themselves, are built around three sections: "Claim Your Story," "Enter the Bible Story," and "Live the Story." Sessions are designed to move participants from an awareness of their own life story, issues, needs, and experiences into an encounter and dialogue with the story of Scripture and to make decisions integrating their personal stories and the Bible's story.

The session plans in the following pages will provide questions and activities to help your group focus on the particular content of each chapter. In addition to questions and activities, the plans will include chapter title, Scripture, and faith focus.

Here are things to keep in mind for all the sessions:

Prepare Ahead
Study the Scripture, comparing different translations and perhaps a paraphrase.
Read the chapter, and consider what it says about your life and the Scripture.
Gather materials such as large sheets of paper or a markerboard with markers.
Prepare the learning area. Write the faith focus for all to see.

Welcome Participants
Invite participants to greet one another.
Tell them to find one or two people and talk about the faith focus.
Ask: What words stand out for you? Why?

Guide the Session
Look together at "Claim Your Story." Ask participants to give their reactions to the stories and examples given in each chapter. Use questions from the session plan to elicit comments based on personal experiences and insights.

Ask participants to open their Bibles and "Enter the Bible Story." For each portion of Scripture, use questions from the session plan to help participants gain insight into the text and relate it to issues in their own lives.

Step through the activity or questions posed in "Live the Story." Encourage participants to embrace what they have learned and to apply it in their daily lives.

Invite participants to offer their responses or insights about the boxed material in "Across the Testaments," "About the Scripture," and "About the Christian Faith."

Close the Session
Encourage participants to read the following week's Scripture and chapter before the next session.
Offer a closing prayer.

1. God Cares!
Revelation 1–3

Faith Focus
Prayerful worship positions us to hear God speak and perhaps even receive a message from God for others.

Before the Session
Two things for you as group leader to keep in mind:

One, the title of this book is Revelation, singular; it is *not* Revelations, plural. Calling the name of the book in the plural is a very common error.

And two: Do not be afraid of Revelation. Almost all its symbols and allusions are directly out of the Old Testament. The meaning of these symbols and allusions was hidden from the Romans, under whose rule the early Christians lived; but the meaning was clear to those who were familiar with the Hebrew Scriptures.

Try to read the entire Book of Revelation, preferably in one sitting. Pay attention not just to the words, but to your feelings and emotions as you read. Read Revelation with your heart as well as with your mind.

Claim Your Story
Invite the group members to form teams of three persons each and to share with one another in their teams a time or times in their lives when they have felt defeated, disillusioned, and frightened. Don't force anyone to respond who chooses not to do so. Pose these questions also: Were these times over which you had control—or no control? Did the church help you in any way at these times? How did your faith come into play during these times of distress?

Do not take the time to hear reports from the teams; but if a team has a special concern, deal with it.

Enter the Bible Story
One of the classic philosophical arguments against the existence of God goes something like this: If God is all-good and all-powerful, why is there suffering in the world? John, writing on the island of Patmos, probably struggled with this same question. Ask group members to form pairs, review quickly the opening paragraphs under "Enter the Story" in this chapter of the study, and struggle for a moment with that question.

The Imperial Cult
Call the group back together and move to a quick review of the study writers' comments on the imperial cult. Then form the pairs again and ask them to consider if anything in our day is similar to the imperial cult. What demands our attention and allegiance in

competition with our allegiance to God? Ask for a few ideas and post these on a chalkboard or large sheet of paper.

Caesar or Christ?

Review the "Caesar or Christ" section in the study. Then ask the group to answer the three questions posed by the study writers at the end of this section.

A Vision of God's Plan

The study writers point out that God granted John a glimpse of the divine court in heaven. Help group members recognize that Revelation probably was written before the New Testament was established. Where do we get a glimpse of the kingdom of God? (We gain a glimpse of the kingdom of God from the words and parables of Jesus Christ.)

Who Is Jesus Christ?

As a whole group, carefully consider the section in the study titled "Who Is Jesus Christ?" Read aloud Revelation 1:4-7; then post on the chalkboard or large sheet of paper the characteristics of Jesus Christ. Answer questions such as these: Who is Jesus? What has he done for us? What will he do in the future?

High Priest and Divine Warrior

Ask a group member who is a good reader to read aloud Revelation 1:9-16. Think about the images used in this vision; each of the images comes from the Old Testament. Point out as an example how verse 16 is a parallel of Isaiah 49:2. Again, explain that John used Old Testament images that would speak to the early Christians but would seem like nonsense to the Roman authorities. For more examples, refer the class to the chart titled "Old Testament Roots of Revelation Imagery" in Chapter 1 of the study.

Note that the study writers liken Jesus to a "Divine Warrior." Why was this image important to the Christians of the first centuries? What image might we use rather than "warrior" for Christ Jesus?

What Are Christ's Messages?

Move to the messages dispatched to the seven churches. Again, remind group members that seven is a number of completion or totality; therefore, these messages are for all churches, including the present-day church. Have the class review the chart titled "The Messages to the Seven Churches." Then ask: Which of these churches is most like our own congregation? Are we neither hot nor cold? Are we allowing false teachers to move us from our commitment to Christ? Have we lost our original love for one another and all humankind?

Emphasize again that Revelation has a message for us today just as it had for the Christians of the first centuries.

How Can We Understand and Share These Messages?

The study writers note that John "kept hope alive by maintaining the spiritual disciplines of prayer and worship; so he was ready to see Jesus when he appeared with divine messages on the Lord's Day." Ask: In what ways do you practice those two disciplines today? How do they impact your life of faith? How do they help you share the Christian message with others?

Live the Story

Ask each group member to reflect silently on the following question: What fear or anxiety do you need to place before the throne of grace so that Jesus, the Alpha and Omega, can strengthen you to deal with it? Then lead the group in prayer, asking that God will enable each person present to place that fear or anxiety before that throne, trusting that God will help.

Before winding up this session—and each session on Revelation—ask for questions or concerns. Then post these questions or concerns on the chalkboard or large sheet of paper to be considered at appropriate times. Take each question or concern seriously. Keep in mind that some group members may need to unlearn some ideas they have been taught about the Book of Revelation.

2. Wonder, Love, and Praise
Revelation 4–5

Faith Focus
Our response to God's work of renewal and redemption through the Lamb who was slain is to join all creation in a song of praise.

Before the Session
These two chapters of Revelation get into some of the rich imagery of this great book. Remember: Almost all these images in Revelation were taken from the Old Testament. Therefore, while the message of Revelation is timeless, trying to relate Revelation's detailed symbols and images in concrete ways to current events or situations is unnecessary and fruitless. Do not allow your group members to spend their time trying to translate symbols. The enduring message of Revelation is what is important, not the current identification of individual symbols and images.

Claim Your Story
The study writers quote a law professor at Yale University who says that we live in a "culture of disbelief," one that pushes God aside or considers God merely a comforter. This culture tends to de-emphasize social justice. Ask: How do the traditions of group worship counter that culture and the downplaying of social justice? What happens when you catch a glimpse of the glory of almighty God? How is your life transformed by the experience of joining the angels in praise and worship of the Creator?

Enter the Bible Story
In Revelation 4, John has a wonderful experience: seeing heavenly worship occurring. Is John having a dream? a trance? some kind of unconscious awareness? We do not know for certain, but some of your group members might be able to identify in part with John's experience. Ask: Have any of you ever had a dream that was so weird yet so real that you awoke puzzled and a bit frightened? Some group members may want to relate such dreams, but encourage them to do so quickly. Do group members detect uncertain symbols and images—and sometimes people—in these dreams? While we do not know the exact nature of John's condition, what John sees in that state is crucial to Revelation's message.

Regarding the heavenly worship, the study writers raise two issues but say that we need to consider what John sees and hears in order to address them. So mention the issues to the group, but suggest that members wait to address them until later in the session. The two issues are: Why did God allow "John to witness the solemn worship in the heavenly court . . . before showing him the visions of future events . . . ? And how is worship related to the hardship of the church and the destiny of the world?"

Court, Worship, God

John sees a majestic court in heaven, with the throne of God in the center and many fantastic things and worshipers all around. John's vision is a vision of total, ultimate worship. This worship of almighty God involves all the senses. In teams of three, identify those dimensions of the vision in Revelation 4 that relate to seeing, hearing, smelling, tasting, and feeling. Then discuss this question in the teams of three: How does the worship of God in our congregation involve all our senses? Why is involving all the senses in worship important?

Continue to look at this heavenly scene of absolute worship. The study writers suggest that the twenty-four elders represent the twelve tribes of Israel and the twelve apostles of Jesus Christ. Invite the whole group to consider what the four living creatures might represent. (Hint: This question has no right or wrong answer. The four living creatures mean different things to different people; but these creatures, taken from Ezekiel 1, suggest that everything on, under, and above the earth, even those things of which we are not aware, praises God.)

Christ the Lamb

As a whole group, move now to Revelation 5. The scroll contains a detailed description of the future. Who can describe the future accurately? Ask group members to answer this question by looking at Revelation 5:3. What does this say to us today about predictions of the future? Did the people to whom John was writing want to know what would take place in the future? Recall their situation, living as a persecuted minority under Roman dominance. Do we want to know the details of what will take place in the future? Why, or why not? Are we in any way living under the threat of persecution—perhaps of radically different kinds? Identify some of those possible sources of persecution. (Hint: The collapse of social security? The continued threat of terrorism? A global economic depression?)

So what is the answer to the scroll that no one can open? Read Revelation 5:5-10 aloud. Invite group members to identify some of the remarkable contrasts in this description of Jesus Christ. How can Christ at the same time be a lion, the ultimate symbol of power, and a lamb, the ultimate symbol of meekness? How can Christ the Lamb open the scroll if Christ has been "slaughtered"? How is Christ able to open the scroll if no one on earth, in heaven, or under the earth can open it? (Hint: See John 1:1 and John 1:14.) What do these verses from John's Gospel say about Christ? What does Revelation 5 say about Christ?

Believers

Finally, raise this question: What is the final response to all of this in Chapter 5 of Revelation? (Hint: Worship and praise!) What should be our final response to all that takes place in our lives? (Hint: Worship and praise!)

As always, ask for lingering questions and concerns. Post these on a chalkboard or large sheet of paper and deal with these concerns and questions at appropriate times during the session.

Live the Story

As a group, consider the questions posed in the "Live the Story" section of Chapter 2 of the study. Then point out that one of the overall themes of Revelation 4–5 is the unending worship and praise of God. Close this session by worshiping and praising God in the words of Psalm 150. Read this psalm of pure praise aloud as a whole group. Don't worry if group members have different translations; this will just add to the praise! But don't just read the words; use expression and inflection! No one can read the phrase, "loud, clashing cymbals" without shouting God's praises! Praise the Lord!

3. Victory Belongs to God
Revelation 6–11

Faith Focus
God is greater than all troubles, both those real and very present and those imagined in an uncertain future, and will lead the faithful through them.

Before the Session
Read the assigned chapters of Revelation for this session, but don't be surprised if you are confused and overwhelmed. These chapters include some symbolism and images that have given rise to many interpretations. Don't focus on the symbols and miss the main point. Keep asking yourself as you read, *What is the ultimate message in all of this?*

Claim Your Story
Some television preachers proclaim that we are living in the "last days" according to these chapters of Revelation. What do group members think? Point out that many Christians of every generation since the time of the writing of Revelation have believed that they were living in the last days, and probably some members of every generation from now on will believe that they are living in the last days.

Ask a group member to read aloud Matthew 24:36. What does this verse say to those who are confident they know when time will end?

Help group members understand that the purpose of Revelation is not to predict the last days but instead to communicate a significant message to the world.

Read to the group the last paragraph of the "Claim Your Story" section of the study and ask members to respond to the question there.

Enter the Bible Story
Seven seals and seven trumpets—remind the group that seven is a number of completion or totality, as mentioned in Chapter 1 of the study. Remember that seven churches were addressed in the opening chapters of Revelation. Ask group members to look over the paragraphs under "Enter the Bible Story" in this chapter in the study and then have them mention what additional meanings "seven" seems to have.

Opening the Seals
The seals are opened, one by one, by the Lamb. With the opening of the first four, horsemen appear; and the whole earth is subjected to destruction, suffering, and death. Refer group members to the chart "The Four Horsemen of the Apocalypse" in the study.

The study writers raise a question of theodicy: Why must the good suffer along with the evil? This question haunted Job in the Old Testament. Ask: Is there a satisfactory answer to this question?

The study writers remind us of *lex talionis*, that is, the equality of punishment with crime. Pose this question: Is perfect justice ever possible? In seeking perfect justice, how can we avoid escalation (responding in kind but with more intensity)? What is the answer given to the martyrs? Is being told to wait fair? A popular cliché suggests that justice delayed is justice denied. Is this cliché true?

The study writers suggest that the sixth seal provides an answer to this. What is that answer, and does it provide the consolation that the martyrs—and we, when we are waiting for justice—want and need?

Gathering of the Faithful

John sees an angel from the east ready to put a seal on the foreheads of those who serve God. Then John sees a multitude of peoples, each with the seal, everlastingly praising God. In our day, we do not speak of being marked with a seal on our foreheads; but we are sealed nonetheless. Invite group members to consider where that "seal" is upon us. How are we marked as faithful to God? If group members struggle with this issue, refer them to Jeremiah 31:33-34, Matthew 5:8, and Colossians 3:15.

The study writers point out the 144,000 from the 12 tribes of Israel and the unnumbered multitude beyond that—all of whom wear white robes and praise God continuously. Ask: What is suggested by these images? Who is among these faithful servants? Had each of these servants always been faithful to God? Deal with the symbolism of their robes (meaning what?) being "washed in the blood of the Lamb" (again, meaning what?).

Refer group members to the chart "Old Testament Images in Revelation's Gathering of the Faithful."

The study writers point out that the seventh seal introduces a time of reverent silence. Ask: Why are we uncomfortable with silence today? Our homes are filled with radio and television, and even silent prayer in church is uncomfortable for some. Why is this so?

Seven Trumpets Blown

Cataclysmic as the seals were, the seven trumpets introduce even greater pain and suffering. The end seems frighteningly near as each of the first six trumpets introduces even greater anguish. Ask group members to describe the blowing of the seventh trumpet and to identify its message, especially as over against the other six trumpets. What is the overall meaning of the seven seals and the seven trumpets?

The Meaning of the Throne and the Altar

Again, a question of theodicy arises: Why must the good suffer along with the evil? Read Habakkuk 2:2-3 and 2 Peter 3:9. What suggestions do these passages offer? What do these passages say about our impatience and God's timing?

God's Final Victory

Ask a volunteer to read the material in the "God's Final Victory" section to the group. Ask: What help does this message offer today?

Live the Story

As a whole group, identify the overriding message of Revelation 6–11. What do these chapters say about who is in charge? Who gains the victory? What do you think this message meant for those living under severe persecution? What does this message mean for us?

Read aloud Isaiah 43:1-7. Then invite the group members to pray in silence, thanking God for bringing them through calamities.

4. The Endurance of the Saints
Revelation 12–14

Faith Focus
Evil is real and battles goodness; but in the end, God and those who stand with God win.

Before the Session
The calamities that befell the earth through the seals and trumpets were to some extent unavoidable. Here, the calamities are the result of human sinfulness, personified by dragons and beasts. Read Revelation 12–14 and Chapter 4 in the study. Remember that Revelation was written for people living under horrible persecution.

Claim Your Story
Remind group members that these chapters are full of dragons and beasts. In teams of four consider these questions: Have you, a family member, or a friend ever fought a dragon or a beast? If the teams seem slow to respond, suggest that various kinds of addictions could be beasts and dragons. Worry, anxiety, and depression may be beasts and dragons. What other kinds of dragons and beasts can the teams identify?

Enter the Bible Story
Satan, Mother, and Child
These chapters in Revelation commence with the story of the woman about to give birth and the dragon that stood ready to devour the infant. Realize that the characters in these chapters are symbols. Recall the story of Eve and the snake in the garden of Eden. How is this story different from the story of Eve in the garden? Deal with this question: What has transpired between the time of Eve and the serpent and the time of this woman and the dragon? Hint: Think in terms of who helped Eve and who helped this woman.

Fighting in Heaven
As a whole group, discuss the battle in heaven, using these questions:

1. Why does John identify the angel Michael, already known to the readers of Revelation as the protector of God's people (see Daniel 12:1)?
2. Where are Satan and Satan's angels at the time of this heavenly battle?
3. Satan and Satan's warriors are thrown out of heaven, but what does the fact that they were in heaven to begin with say about God and Creation? (Hint: Nothing exists that was not created by God, including the heavenly beings that became Satan and Satan's warriors.)

4. What forms do Satan and Satan's warriors take once thrown to earth? Think: Are they external, outside us?
5. Or are they within us? Give reasons for your answers.

Danger on Earth

Once on earth, Satan seeks to make war on the woman who has just given birth. Ask: Who or what might the woman and the child represent here? The woman is protected from Satan by the eagle and the drying up of the river. In reality, who or what saved the woman and all that she represents?

As a result of these interventions, Satan determines to make war on the rest of the children of earth. Ask: How does Satan make war on us today? Can we always recognize Satan, or does Satan wear many disguises? If so, name some of these disguises. How is our own rebellion against God involved?

The Beast From the Sea

Ask: Who or what is represented by the beast from the sea? While debates rage over just who this beast represents, challenge your group members to struggle with the meaning of this beast. Put most simply, evil, represented by the dragon and Satan, engenders more evil. Evil creates and attracts more evil. Ask group members to cite some examples of this reality.

The Beast From the Land

Again, scholars debate the possible identity of the beast from the land; but here is another example of sinfulness breeding more sin. If the beast from the land is the Roman Empire and if the Empire forced people to worship the emperor, then the Roman Empire was pushing sin. Ask: Are we encouraged to worship anything but God in our day? What are some of the things that people worship today? What encourages them to undertake this worship? Is this worship always overt and intentional, or is this worship subtle and unintentional but worship of an idol nonetheless. Ask for examples to support answers.

Entertain questions or comments about the number 666. Refer to the study for a possible interpretation of this number.

The Lamb and the 144,000

The scene changes. Surrounding the Lamb are 144,000 persons with the name of the Lamb written on their foreheads. Again, where is the name of God written upon us? Are we among the righteous? How can we know? The study writers refer to these 144,000 as the first fruits of a great harvest. Ask: What part do we play in the harvest to come?

Messages From Three Angels

Ask: What are the three statements made by the three angels? What relevance do these statements have for us in the twenty-first century? Do these statements refer to all persons at all times? Again, give reasons for answers.

Two Harvests

What is the message of the two harvests? Is judgment absolutely inevitable? How can we prepare for the harvests and be sure we are harvested with the righteous?

Live the Story

Ask a volunteer to read aloud the "Live the Story" section from the study. Then ask class members to share their reactions.

Offer a prayer of thanksgiving that God is still in control.

5. God's Judgments Are Just
Revelation 15–16

Faith Focus
When we look to God for help, times of chaos can be opportunities to pursue a God-blessed course.

Before the Session
In these two chapters of Revelation, the symbols and images flow fast and furiously. Keep in mind that John was writing to Christians in the Roman Empire who were suffering horribly for their faith. Is it not human nature to cry out for justice and silently—and sometimes not so silently—wish ill on your tormenters?

Be prepared for questions and comments from group members around these two chapters, and take every question or comment seriously.

Claim Your Story
While the writers of the study remind us of the horror of the Civil War, most of your group members will remember the day airplanes flew into the twin towers of the World Trade Center, into the Pentagon, and into a field in Pennsylvania in a thwarted attempt to attack the White House. Ask the group members to recall their feelings and attitudes when the man considered responsible for this attack was himself attacked and killed in 2011. Was justice served? Were the celebrations that took place in the United States at the time of Osama bin Laden's death warranted? If celebration was not appropriate, what emotions should faithful people feel at such a time?

Enter the Bible Story
The Song of Moses and the Lamb
Invite group members in teams of four to read the section in the study titled "The Song of Moses and the Lamb" and then to read Exodus 15:1-18. Note differences in these two songs of triumph. Pay special attention to Revelation 15:4. Hear reports from a few of the teams. Do all detect the significance of the statement, "all nations will come and fall down in worship before you"?

Plagues Against Pharaoh and Caesar
The study writers point out the parallels between this scene and details in the Exodus story. (Refer the group to the chart titled "The Wrath of God in the Old and New Testaments.") Recall that these parallels meant nothing to the Roman authorities but were very meaningful to the suffering Christians in Rome. Discuss the significance of these parallels. What did they mean to the Christians to whom John was writing? What do these parallels mean to us today?

Plagues of Sores and Blood

The first three bowls of wrath are almost direct parallels to the plagues that haunted Egypt when Moses was demanding the release of the Hebrew slaves. Again, what is the significance of this parallelism? These plagues of judgment are called "true and just." Who is making the judgments? Are our judgments always true and just? Or is it only God's judgments that are true and just? Give reasons for answering as you do.

Plagues of Heat, Darkness, and Drought

The next plagues are again parallels of the plagues that affected Pharaoh and the people of Egypt during the time of Moses. What are the results of these plagues, both in Exodus and here in Revelation? How are the people who worship the beast like—and unlike—Pharaoh? Address a larger question: Why do people, even in our day, curse God and refuse to repent? What will cause such people to repent if even great suffering does not do so?

John sees froglike demonic spirits. Are demonic spirits afoot in our world today? If so, what forms do these demonic spirits take?

Review the study writers' comments about Armageddon in the main text and in the sidebar "Armageddon." If any members of your group have visited Israel, encourage them to describe the Plain of Jezreel and the valley and mountain of Megiddo.

A Plague of Lightning, Thunder, and Earthquake

The seventh bowl is perhaps the most devastating. God's justice is finally served completely, and the places of great sinfulness and godlessness are destroyed. Again, what was the response of the sinful? Why did they not repent even in the face of all this devastation? Raise this question: Are some people simply beyond repentance? Is it ever too late to repent, or is repentance always possible?

Live the Story

Ask a volunteer to read the "Live the Story" section from the study. Then spend a few moments with the questions the study writers raise at the end of that section.

Next, tell the group that almost every person who ever lived has experienced what could be described as an injustice. Ask group members to assume an attitude of prayer. Then read each of the following statements aloud, leaving time for reflection between each one:

1. Recall a time when you suffered what you believed to be an injustice at the hands of another.
2. Was the injustice ever resolved? If it was resolved, how was it resolved and who resolved it?
3. When should you leave vengeance and recompense to God? What do you need to do to step away from seeking revenge?

Pray for all who suffer injustice of any kind. Affirm that God is still in control.

6. Loose and Extravagant Ways
Revelation 17–18

Faith Focus
The way that runs counter to God's way is tempting and attractive, but it leads to destruction. God's way leads to life.

Before the Session
The symbolism and imagery of Revelation continues, but in these two chapters the antecedents of many of the symbols are obvious. Almost all commentators equate the woman and Babylon with the city of Rome. Similarly, most commentators equate the "kings" in Revelation 17 with Roman emperors and governors, culminating in Nero.

Recall again that Revelation was written for a particular, persecuted people at a particular time. It was written in a kind of a code, that is, Old Testament images that were comprehensible to the Christians but meaningless to the Roman authorities.

Claim Your Story
While the great whore of Chapter 17 of Revelation is usually associated with the sinful city of Rome, the study writers expand the concept to suggest that the woman represents greed, lust, and the passion to acquire things and power, regardless of the cost.

Read aloud the section of the study titled "Claim Your Story." Then ask the whole group to comment on questions such as these: Are we living in a materialistic, lustful society? What transpires in our culture that feeds our materialism and lust for things?

If the group struggles with this issue, help them think about the power of advertising. Much advertising tells us that we are incomplete, imperfect, less than we should be, and that by purchasing and using this or that product, we will become complete, more nearly perfect, and more nearly what we should be. Does this mean that advertising is sinful? What is the responsibility of the Christian when bombarded with advertising?

Enter the Bible Story
The Woman Named Babylon and the Beast
The study writers talk about those who have been seduced by power and wealth. Ask: In what ways do power and wealth still seduce us? Why are so few of us content with what we have? What compels many of us always to lust for more?

How does all of this pertain to Christians? What is Jesus' statement about this? Does all of this mean that no person can be a committed Christian and also be wealthy by worldly standards? Give reasons for your answers.

Seven Hills and Seven Kings
Help the group recognize that the seven kings and the ten additional kings are Roman emperors and governors. Refer members to the chart in the study titled "The Kings

(Emperors) of Rome." Ask: How long did these emperors and governors last? Then read aloud the conclusion of the angel's announcement, Revelation 17:14. What does this say to those in our day and age who are seduced by wealth, power, and prestige? Why is the lure of materialism described as seduction? As Christ was envisioned as destroying the oppressive military and economic power of Rome in the first century, might Christ destroy oppressive military and economic powers today? Give reasons for answering as you do.

Turmoil in Rome

The study writers point out that subjecting a people to dishonest and prideful rulers will lead to revolt (see Revelation 17:16). Ask: When in recent history have we seen a people in revolt against unjust and abusive rulers?

The Fall of Babylon

The angel announces not just the fall of Babylon, but the complete destruction of Babylon (Rome). Ask: Why can't injustice, greed, avarice, and pride be self-sustaining over a long period of time? Why must God intervene in human history and destroy such forces? What means does God use to destroy them?

Mourning by Kings, Merchants, and Seafarers

Ask: What insight do we gain from the three groups that bewail the fall of Babylon? Are we in our time as interdependent as the kings, merchants, and seafarers were interdependent with Rome? Give examples to support your answer. Then pose this question: Is the fact that we live in a global, interdependent economy in and of itself positive or negative? Again, provide reasons for answering as you do.

The End of an Era

Discuss as a whole group: Is our nation and our world in any danger of being as "thrown down" as was Babylon/Rome? If so, then what are we as individuals called to do and to be?

Live the Story

One of the central themes of Revelation 17–18 is that the way that runs counter to God's way is tempting and attractive, but it leads to destruction. Ask a volunteer to read the final paragraph of the "Live the Story" section of Chapter 6 in the study. Then ask the group: Do you agree with the study writers that "we express our beliefs every time we open our wallets"? Why, or why not?

These chapters also tell us that God's judgment is sure. Yet at the same time, a predominant theme is that God takes care of God's own and God's grace and mercy is everlasting.

Invite each group member to do this: Jot down on a slip of paper—for her or his eyes only—at least one vital learning gained from these two chapters in Revelation that will positively affect the way he or she lives. Encourage group members to keep their slips of paper in pocket or purse and to refer to these learnings often in the week ahead.

7. God Is in Control

Revelation 19–20

Faith Focus

When we are in the midst of trouble or have been victimized, it seems small comfort to say that evildoers will get their comeuppance; but they will, and in the end, holding fast to God brings real comfort.

Before the Session

Some in your group may be growing somewhat troubled by the mysterious events in Revelation. Be prepared to remind folks that the message of Revelation is that God wins in the end; and because God wins, those who profess their faith in God and live out that faith also triumph. Remind group members that all of life has its "ups and downs," that no life is a straight line toward completion.

Claim Your Story

Ask a volunteer to read aloud the "Claim Your Story" section in the study. Invite group members to comment on the story of Michael Vick. Do you find his post-prison testimony convincing? Why, or why not?

Then ask: Are there any points at which your own story leads to a similar testimony?

Finally, read aloud again the last sentence in the "Claim Your Story" section. Then ask group members if they agree with it and if so, under what conditions?

Enter the Bible Story

Revelation 19 begins with a song of praise that the great prostitute has been thrown down. Encourage group members to continue reading Chapter 19, for the tone changes from rejoicing over the fall of the prostitute to praise of God. Ask: When is celebrating the defeat of an enemy appropriate? How can we praise God without gloating over the overthrow of those who are unrighteous?

The Lamb and His Bride

The study writers say the Lamb is Christ and the bride is the church. Ask: What church is being described here? How can any congregation be sure that it is participating in the true church that is married to the Lamb? In your congregation, who are the "saints" whose "acts of justice" assure you that your church is part of the bride of Christ?

Discuss in teams of three: Who is invited to the marriage banquet of the Lamb? How can we know if we have been invited?

The angel demands that John not worship the angel but worship only God. Ask: What might we be tempted to worship besides—or in place of—God?

Christ Defeats the Beast and His Armies

Christ, once appearing in the meekness of a lamb, now appears on a white horse, the symbol of military might. The study writers refer to Christ as the Divine Warrior. Ask: How can we conceive of Christ as both the sacrificial Lamb and the Divine Warrior? What is unique about the warfare that Christ conducts? Hint: See the second half of Revelation 19:11.

Who are they in white robes that go into battle with Christ? Are we numbered among them? Are we engaging in just and righteous battles for Christ? Does battle imagery even work as a metaphor for serving Christ in this day and age?

Discuss as a whole group: Why is one of Christ's names hidden? Why does Christ have so many names? If the group struggles with this question, ask: Can any one name summarize all that Christ is and does?

Again, as a whole group: Why are the birds of prey eating the flesh of the sinful kings? Think broadly: What does this image suggest? Similarly, the beast and the false prophet are thrown into a lake burning with sulfur. What does this image suggest?

Satan Is Confined

The hurling of Satan into the abyss is one of several climatic events in these latter chapters of Revelation. The study writers point out that Christians do not agree on the meaning of the thousand years; and denominations have split over premillennialism, amillennialism, and postmillennialism. But invite your group to consider the real point of this hurling down of Satan. What is John seeing and discovering through this vision? What is God saying to John through this event? What for us is the meaning of even Satan being given a second chance?

The Saints Come to Life and Reign With Christ

Discuss as a whole group: What is the meaning of the "second death"? Should committed Christians be concerned with the second death? Why, or why not? How might John's vision be helpful to Christians being threatened with martyrdom?

Satan Is Defeated

Satan fails at the second chance and is cast into the lake of fire. Consider: Does this suggest that we may run out of chances? Ask a group member to read Luke 13:6-9 aloud. How does this parable from Jesus address this question?

The Final Judgment

The Final Judgment involves opening scrolls to judge what each person has done. Do you think God actually "keeps score" of each of our wrongs? How else might this imagery of opened scrolls be interpreted? What is the basic message here?

Live the Story

These chapters are the story of God's ultimate triumph and of those who will triumph with God over the forces of evil and sinfulness. Invite group members to a time of silent reflection as you read these questions aloud:

What does God's ultimate victory mean for you, personally?
How does this ultimate victory influence the way you move into the future?
In what ways does Christ's offer of forgiveness and peace help you live each day?
How does the assurance of God's ultimate victory change the way you live today?

Close with the whole group praying the Lord's Prayer.

8. All Things New

Revelation 21–22

Faith Focus

As followers of Jesus, we are on the road to where everything is made new and forever trouble-free—Eden restored!

Before the Session

We come to the last two chapters of Revelation. Here you will find some of the most moving and beautiful passages of Scripture in the Bible. Not only are the word pictures painted by John in these two chapters marvelous, the promise and assurances described in these chapters are yours and your group members' to claim as your own.

Read the chapter in the study and the two chapters from Revelation. Read for the meaning and the message.

Pray for each of your group members by name. Pray that each group member might discover new truth in the Scriptures and may live out that truth triumphantly.

Claim Your Story

Invite group members to share the times and places they have heard some of the words of Revelation 21 and 22. Call to mind hymns and gospel songs that make reference to some of the images used in these chapters.

Expect some group members to recall that parts of these two chapters are often read at funerals. *The United Methodist Book of Worship* labels funerals as "Services of Death and Resurrection." Ask group members why that is a good description for the funeral of a Christian.

Ask further: Do these two chapters from Revelation refer only to life after physical death? Or can these chapters in some way describe life here and now? Encourage group members to give reasons and examples for their answers.

Enter the Bible Story

Read aloud the first two sentences from this chapter in the study in the section titled "Enter the Bible Story." These sentences sum up these two chapters of Revelation precisely; and this session will be devoted to defining that new relationship, the original creation that is restored, and the divine-human covenant God has put back in place despite the sinfulness and apostasy of humankind. Therefore, invite group members to define the new relationship, the restored original creation, and the divine-human covenant. Jot their definitions on a chalkboard or large sheet of paper.

New Heaven, New Earth

The study writers remind us that the words of the beginning of Revelation 21 describe a new covenant between God and God's people, a covenant initiated by God. As a whole group, discuss the meaning of covenant. How is a covenant different from and much more than a contract? With whom is God making this new covenant?

Next, use this section of the study to trace some of the Old Testament images within this new covenant. In what ways does the entire biblical story lead up to this new covenant?

New Jerusalem

John is taken on a tour of New Jerusalem, and he finds it glorious beyond his greatest expectations. While we may not think of heaven as streets of gold and pearls for gates, the study writers point out that these are symbols of our relationship with God. Ask: What symbols might we use today as symbols of our enduring relationship with God? Would we still use golden streets and gigantic pearls? Why, or why not? What particular symbols remind us that we are God's people?

In groups of two, have group members read Revelation 21 and list what else is new in New Jerusalem.

No Temple in New Jerusalem

Ask: Why is there no temple in New Jerusalem? What do temples and churches represent? Why, then, is none needed in New Jerusalem? In teams of three, consider this question: How do you feel about the prospect of seeing God face-to-face? Does that frighten or excite you? Why?

Jesus Is Coming Soon

John sees and hears in his vision that Jesus is coming soon. But Jesus has not yet come, and almost two thousand years have passed since John's vision. Ask: What do you make of this? How soon is "soon"? But much more importantly: How are we to live in the anticipation of the second coming of Jesus? Do we know and live the words of Scripture?

Testify!

Note how the images of Revelation often point to water. This is understandable in a land that is arid and filled with desert wildernesses. Invite group members to think of symbols of today that might be used in place of water. What is as central to our lives as pure water was to the people of John's time?

Notice in Revelation how the angel testifies, John testifies, Jesus the Christ testifies. In what ways are we called to testify, and what is the message we proclaim as we testify? Can we proclaim God's promise that Eden will be restored? How does the way we live our lives bear testimony to that promise?

Live the Story

Pose these questions for silent reflection by the group members: Is the new heaven and new earth that John described something we will discover only after physical death? If your answer is no, then how can we experience all of this here and now?

Ask group members to read silently the section in their study books titled "Live the Story." Then invite group members to share sentence prayers of thanksgiving for their study of the Book of Revelation.

Made in the USA
Coppell, TX
18 March 2022

Also by Mary Kathleen Benet

The Secretarial Ghetto

The Politics of Adoption